Entrepreneur. **STARTUP**

START YOUR OWN

Virtual
Assistant
Business

YOUR STEP-BY-STEP GUIDE
TO SUCCESS

THE STAFF OF ENTREPRENEUR MEDIA
AND JASON R. RICH

Entrepreneur Press®

Publisher: Entrepreneur Press
Cover Design: Andrew Welyczko
Production and Composition: Eliot House Productions

This publication is designed to provide accurate and authoritative information in regard to the subject matter covered. It is sold with the understanding that the publisher is not engaged in rendering legal, accounting, or other professional services. If legal advice or other expert assistance is required, the services of a competent professional person should be sought.

Entrepreneur Press® is a registered trademark of Entrepreneur Media, Inc.

Library of Congress Cataloging-in-Publication Data
  Names: Rich, Jason, author. | Entrepreneur Media, Inc., author.
  Title: Start your own virtual assistant business : your step-by-step guide to success / the Staff of
    Entrepreneur Media, Inc. & Jason R. Rich.
  Description: 1 Edition. | Irvine : Entrepreneur Press, [2022] | Series: Start your own | Includes index.
  Identifiers: LCCN 2022037015 (print) | LCCN 2022037016 (ebook) | ISBN 9781642011142 (trade
    paperback) | ISBN 9781613084380 (epub)
  Subjects: LCSH: Small business—Management. | Entrepreneurship. | Intelligent personal assistants
    (Computer software) | Success in business.
  Classification: LCC HD62.7 .R534 2022 (print) | LCC HD62.7 (ebook) | DDC 658.022 $2 23/
    eng/20220815—dcundefined
  LC record available at https://lccn.loc.gov/2022037015LC ebook record available at https://lccn.loc.
    gov/2022037016

Printed in the United States of America

27 26 25 24 23   10 9 8 7 6 5 4 3 2 1

START YOUR OWN

Virtual Assistant Business

Additional titles in **Entrepreneur's Startup Series**

Start Your Own

Contents

Chapter 5

Setting Your Pricing 71

Chapter 6

Marketing Your Business to Find Clients 89

Preface

Before the COVID-19 pandemic, working remotely was a privilege enjoyed by only a tiny percentage of the work force, even though it's viable for many types of jobs. But during 2020 and 2021, a significant number of American workers were forced to work remotely—at least for a while. At the same time, previously popular jobs within corporate America became almost extinct, while others prospered in this new remote working environment.

While virtual assistants, as we know them today, have been around as long as the internet, these positions are now more diverse in terms of their responsibilities and more widely accepted than ever. In 2021 and beyond, working as a virtual assistant (or VA) is a prosperous career path for those choosing to pursue this line of work. *Start Your Own Virtual Assistant Business* offers a comprehensive look at what it takes to become a successful virtual assistant.

Every day, clients hire virtual assistants to complete a broad range of both common and highly specialized tasks. If you have specialized skills and/or experience in writing, bookkeeping/accounting, social media marketing, web design, travel planning/coordination, telemarketing, executive administration, data entry, booking appointments/scheduling, project management, database management, or research, for example, you can earn a higher income than a VA who handles more general or administrative tasks for clients. As a virtual assistant, set yourself apart from your competition by developing a niche.

▶ What Is a Virtual Assistant?

A virtual assistant is someone with a specific skill set who works for their clients as an independent contractor. The VA usually works from a home office, relying on online collaboration and communication tools to complete their assignments. Originally, VAs were used mainly for general administrative office work, but these days, people with specialized skills often tackle a much broader range of tasks for their clients. The most successful VAs tend to offer a niche set of skills (such as scheduling, bookkeeping, writing, or social media marketing) to clients in a specific field or industry.

Cindy Opong, founder of Creative Assistants, explained, "In my opinion, the role of a virtual assistant is to support and, in some cases, run the back end of a client's business, so they can focus their time and effort on what they're really good at. I personally specialize in working with [former] top-level executives with corporations who are now starting or running their own consulting business. These people were used to having an executive assistant in the corporate space, and many don't know how to handle core tasks that an executive assistant would typically handle. I come in and I take up that role remotely for them."

Diana Ennen, founder of Virtual Word Publishing, added, "The role of the virtual assistant has changed a lot over the years, and it continues to evolve. A VA is someone the client can rely on to remotely handle specific tasks that are assigned to them. VAs work together with their clients as a partner, helping them to succeed. Often, the client is super busy and needs someone to help ease their workload. I get really involved with my clients' businesses, and I develop strong, long-lasting business relationships with them."

After explaining the many benefits and responsibilities of becoming a virtual assistant, this book will help you determine if this line of work is suitable for you and is something you're qualified for. If so, it will also help you establish a strong foundation as you launch your business.

Later chapters explain in detail how to find, land, and manage clients. Plus, you'll learn how to create a home office environment that will help you become and stay productive. After branding your business, you'll discover tricks for successfully promoting it without spending a fortune. You'll also learn how to avoid or overcome some common pitfalls of working as a virtual assistant and how to manage the day-to-day operation of what will hopefully become a highly profitable part-time or even full-time business venture.

The amount virtual assistants charge for their services varies tremendously, from around $10 to upward of $100 per hour, depending on the tasks being done, the VA's qualifications and experience, and the type of client they are working with. This book will help position you toward the higher end of that scale, once you've gained some real-world experience.

This Book Offers a Plethora of Advice from Experts

If you were to ask almost any CEO or business leader for advice about how to get started and become successful in a specific line of work, chances are you'd be told to find a mentor and learn as much as possible from their guidance. While you might not yet have direct access to already successful and highly experienced virtual assistants to seek advice from in person, this book offers in-depth, exclusive, and highly informative interviews with several successful and well-established virtual assistants.

The people featured in this book all generously shared their insights, experience, advice, and personal anecdotes in a way you can directly benefit from as you pursue a career as a virtual assistant and begin establishing your own virtual assistant business. By including VAs with a

fun fact ☺

A virtual assistant agency is a company that serves as the middleman between clients and virtual assistants. The agency is hired to do work by clients, which it then subcontracts out to qualified VAs (who work either as independent contractors or employees for that agency). The agency handles tasks like finding new clients, client onboarding, setting rates, and billing on behalf of the virtual assistants. Many agencies also provide training and professional networking opportunities to the VAs it works with. Some people find that working for a virtual assistant agency is a good way to break into this field.

wide range of backgrounds, who cater to clients in specific niches, and who are located throughout the world, we've given you access to many divergent opinions and points of view. You'll also read interviews with people who operate virtual assistant agencies and small business owners who are thriving with the help of their virtual assistants, so you can learn from their perspectives as well.

Their advice can help you avoid time-consuming and potentially costly mistakes as you get started.

Facts You Need to Know Upfront

For the right type of person, becoming a virtual assistant can be a highly lucrative, fun, challenging, and rewarding career path that has few barriers for entry and tremendous potential for growth. However, it is not a "get rich quick" scheme. You'll only succeed if you put in the necessary planning and preparation, combined with patience, creativity, hard work, and dedication.

fun fact ☺

Being a virtual assistant offers independence. You can be your own boss, control your own schedule, and work from home. Once you're in demand, you'll likely be able to pick and choose your clients. Plus, it's easy to get started: The startup costs are very low, and for the most part no special licenses or degrees are required.

► **Research from the Association of Virtual Assistants**

In 2020, the Association of Virtual Assistants (https://associationofvas.com/) conducted a survey of more than 500 working virtual assistants for its "VA State of the Industry Report." In the survey, 93 percent of respondents said they "enjoy[ed] freedom and flexibility" working as VAs.

The report also found that 38 percent of respondents worked 20 to 30 hours per week, while 26 percent said they worked more than 40 hours, 24 percent worked 10 to 20 hours, and 11 percent worked 1 to 10 hours.

When it came to hourly rates, the report stated that 58 percent of virtual assistants earn $26 to $50 per hour, 23 percent earn $10 to $25 per hour, 18 percent earn $51 to $100 per hour, and just 1 percent earn more than $100 per hour.

In terms of monthly income, 33 percent reported making between $2,001 and $5,000 per month, 26 percent made between $1,001 and $2,000, 16 percent made between $0 and $500, 14 percent made between $551 and $1,000, and 11 percent made more than $5,000. You'll learn more about the Association of Virtual Assistants in an interview with its founder and CEO, Melissa Smith, in Chapter 6.

In upcoming chapters, you'll learn about the knowledge, specialized skills, and personality traits you will need to become a successful virtual assistant in your particular niche. But there are some qualities all VAs must have that you should know about upfront: an outgoing personality, top-notch written and verbal communication skills, the ability to multitask, excellent time management skills, confidence, a dash of creativity, and proven problem-solving abilities.

In addition, high proficiency with PCs, the internet, and software—including messaging apps, videoconferencing apps, popular office suites (like Microsoft Office, Microsoft 365, and Google Workspace), and the remote collaboration tools built into these widely used apps—are absolutely necessary. Being able to collaborate with others (located in different locations) using Microsoft Word or Excel, for example, has become a required task for virtual workers. This is all on top of your proficiency at the specialized tasks your clients hire you to complete, whether that's bookkeeping, web design, or marketing.

So if the idea of becoming a part-time or full-time virtual assistant sounds intriguing, *Start Your Own Virtual Assistant Business* will give you a comprehensive overview of how to get started and succeed!

Becoming a Virtual Assistant

A virtual assistant is someone who works as an independent contractor, typically from a home office, for one or more clients, and who handles specific tasks assigned by their clients.

As you'll discover in Chapter 2, those tasks can vary greatly. Each VA's role depends on the unique skill set, experience, and preferences of the person doing the work.

While some VAs promote themselves as a jack-of-all-trades who can handle any type of administrative work, for example, they often receive much less money in return for their labor. The ones who offer a niche set of services to a very specific clientele are usually able to charge the highest rates. Once you've decided to become a VA, it's important to determine your skill set and narrow down the types of clients your experience and expertise will most appeal to.

Choose a Pricing Model for Your Work

There are several pricing models that VAs typically use, so select the one that makes the most sense for you and your client(s):

- ▶ *A set hourly rate.* Clients can pay for as many hours of work as they need, as they're needed. VAs who focus on individual projects for clients, as opposed to working on a retainer and maintaining an ongoing relationship, tend to go with this option. A client may either pay for the VA's time upfront or be billed after the work is completed.
- ▶ *Prepaid blocks of hours.* These blocks could be 5, 10, 15, or 20 hours per month, but the client gets a discount on the VA's usual hourly rate for paying in advance. Often, unused hours do not roll over to the following month. If a client needs more work done, they're charged a specified hourly rate for the additional time.
- ▶ *A per-project basis.* Here, the project's details and deadline are spelled out in the contract and the client pays a flat fee to the VA, regardless of how many hours it takes to complete the work. The client may pay 50 percent upfront, with the balance due upon completion.

VAs use several other pricing models as well—we'll talk about them in Chapter 5.

VAs Typically Work from a Home Office

One of the biggest benefits of being a virtual assistant is that your location rarely matters to your clients, as long as you're accessible during their business hours and finish your work on time. However, some clients do prefer VAs who live and work in their time zone, even though they may never meet in person.

Working as an independent contractor from your home office makes you your own boss. You set your rates, determine the number of hours you're willing to work each week, and create your daily schedule.

As a business operator, you're also in charge of:

► Finding and managing your clients
► Marketing and promoting your business (online and in the real world)
► Handling the bookkeeping and accounting
► Billing (and collecting on overdue invoices)
► Keeping your skill set up-to-date
► Meeting your deadlines

Running a VA Business Makes You the Boss

As a virtual assistant, you are a small business owner. This means you must set up your business as a legal entity right from the start and then pay state and federal taxes on your income.

When starting out, most VAs establish their business as a *sole proprietorship*. This is the easiest and least expensive option. However, some choose to establish their business as a *limited liability company* (LLC), or once it becomes successful, they transform their sole proprietorship into an LLC. Before deciding on your legal entity, consult with an accountant and/or lawyer who specializes in small business startups.

► Some VAs Work with an Agency

A *virtual assistant agency* is a company that serves as the middleman between clients and virtual assistants. The agency typically finds and manages the VA's clients, handles the company's marketing, sets the VA's rates, handles the invoicing and bookkeeping, and in some cases, offers specialized training for the virtual assistants working for them. Another benefit for a VA who chooses to work with an agency is that they gain access to an instant network of other VAs who can serve as mentors and potentially friends.

For some, working for an agency is the perfect way to learn how to become a virtual assistant and gain real-world work experience, instead of having to manage all aspects of their own business.

As you'll see later, the main drawback to working for a VA agency is the lower pay. Because the agency handles the management and back-end side of the business, it's paid a large commission on what you earn from your clients.

The Differences Between a Sole Proprietorship and Limited Liability Company

According to the SBA's website, "A sole proprietorship is the simplest and most common structure chosen to start a business. It is an unincorporated business owned and run by one individual with no distinction between the business and you, the owner. You are entitled to all profits and are responsible for all your business's debts, losses, and liabilities."

You don't need to do anything specific to form a sole proprietorship, provided that you are the only owner. However, you must still acquire a business license and/or permits, based on the location where you'll be operating and the industry your clients will be working in. Regulations vary by industry, state, and locality.

Keep in mind, if you opt to create a company name instead of just operating your business under your own name, it's typically required that you file a DBA (doing business as) document with your local or state government. A DBA is also required to open a business bank account under your company name.

> **tip**
>
> You also might want to protect your unique business name by applying for a trademark with the U.S. Patent and Trademark Office (www.uspto.gov).

Filing a DBA is very easy and inexpensive. You can do it yourself online by filing the appropriate forms with your local government. For state-specific instructions, search online for "File for a DBA in [insert your state]." A fee-based service, such as LegalZoom (https://www.legalzoom.com/sem/biz/dba.html), can handle this task for you for a flat fee (under $120).

According to the SBA, "Because you and your business are one and the same, the business itself is not taxed separately. The sole proprietorship income is your income. You report income and/or losses and expenses with a Schedule C and the standard Form 1040 when filing your taxes. The 'bottom-line amount' from the Schedule C transfers to your personal tax return. It's your responsibility to withhold and pay all income taxes, including self-employment and estimated taxes."

The biggest drawback to operating a sole proprietorship is that there is no legal separation between you and your business. The SBA notes, "You can be held personally liable for the debts and obligations of the business. This risk extends to any liabilities incurred as a result of employee actions."

The primary alternative to a sole proprietorship is a limited liability company, or LLC. This offers some additional legal protections but also requires you to file your personal and business-related tax returns slightly differently. Doing this will require you to file your personal tax returns differently, involves higher setup costs, and typically involves hiring a lawyer and/or accountant to establish this type of business.

According to the IRS, "A limited liability company (LLC) is a business structure allowed by state statute. Each state may use different regulations, so you should check with your state if you are interested in starting a limited liability company. Owners of an LLC are called members. Most states do not restrict ownership, so members may include individuals, corporations, other LLCs, and foreign entities. There is no maximum number of members.

"Most states also permit 'single-member' LLCs, those having only one owner . . . The IRS will treat an LLC as either a corporation, partnership, or as part of the LLC's owner's tax return (a 'disregarded entity'). For income tax purposes, an LLC with only one member is treated as an entity disregarded as separate from its owner, unless it files Form 8832 and elects to be treated as a corporation. However, for purposes of employment tax and certain excise taxes, an LLC with only one member is still considered a separate entity."

> **tip**
>
> One possible legal requirement when you establish a virtual assistant business may be to obtain an Employer Identification Number (EIN) for your business. This will depend on several factors, such as your location and the type of business entity you choose. For more information about acquiring an EIN for your business, visit www.irs.gov/businesses.

As a self-employed independent contractor, you are required to file an annual tax return, but you must also pay quarterly estimated state and federal taxes, based on your income. You'll also have to pay self-employment tax, which is associated with Social Security and Medicare. Determining whether you're subject to self-employment tax will require you to calculate the net profit and loss from your business.

Accounting/bookkeeping software, such as QuickBooks (https://quickbooks.intuit.com), can help you maintain proper financial records, although you may prefer to work with a professional bookkeeper or accountant. Even if you choose to hire professional help, you will want to manage your company's finances using software that your accountant also supports.

If you're on a tight budget at first and hiring an accountant is not possible, look into the free business mentors available through SCORE (https://www.score.org/find-mentor). With more than 10,000 volunteers throughout the United States, SCORE is a nonprofit organization that offers free business mentoring advice to startups and established small businesses.

Once you determine how you'll set up your business, you can obtain and file the necessary paperwork yourself, hire an attorney to do it for you, or work with an independent company such as LegalZoom. A service like LegalZoom costs less than a lawyer but does not provide the advice you might need to make appropriate decisions.

VAs Always Need to Multitask

Above and beyond the everyday tasks your clients assign, your responsibilities include the day-to-day operation of your own business. Juggling all these tasks requires a high level of organization, along with time management, project management, bookkeeping, customer service, and multitasking skills.

There is a wide range of software, online, and mobile app-based tools that can help you organize your time, assist with bookkeeping, and make managing multiple projects easier. It's your responsibility, however, to choose the best tools for your work habits and then become proficient at using those tools. You'll learn more about some of these tools within Chapter 4 and Chapter 8.

Running a VA business also requires top-notch written and verbal communication skills. While you may never meet your clients in person, you will likely be regularly speaking with them on the phone, engaging in video calls (virtual meetings) with them, and frequently exchanging emails and text messages.

How you'll communicate with your clients, and how often, is typically agreed to at the beginning of the working relationship. The specific communication tools you'll use

aha!

Grammarly (www.grammarly.com/) is a software, mobile app, and cloud-based tool that proofreads and corrects your writing as you type. This low-cost application works in conjunction with email, text messaging, and word processors, among other mediums, and goes well beyond just checking your work for spelling, grammar, and punctuation errors.

▶ What Are the Education Requirements for Becoming a VA?

The short answer to this question is "none." You don't need a college degree, master's, Ph.D., or even specialized certifications, as long as you can prove to potential clients that you can perform the job you're being hired to do. You *can* justify charging higher rates, however, if you have degrees and/or certifications related to specific skills you'll be using. As a VA, focus on fine-tuning and continuously expanding your marketable skill set, either through in-person or online training. Only about 60 percent of currently employed virtual assistants have a college education.

are typically chosen by the client, based on their already established work flows.

As a result, one client might want you to check in via one voice call per week, while maintaining ongoing communication using the messaging app Slack. Another might prefer video calls via Zoom or Microsoft Teams and the ongoing exchange of emails to stay in touch. You'll need to become proficient at all these communication tools and learn how to communicate clearly, succinctly, and efficiently.

warning

Poor or inadequate communication between a VA and their client often leads to mistakes or misunderstandings that cost time and even money to fix. It can also easily tarnish your professional reputation and cause you to lose clients.

VAs Typically Get to Choose Their Own Clients

One of the biggest benefits of running your own virtual assistant business is that you get to choose the types of clients you want to work for (based on the skills you have and the work you're able and willing to do).

Initially, as you're just starting out, you might be less picky and take on any client who's willing to pay you. Eventually, however, you'll have the luxury of turning away clients you think aren't a good fit. Likewise, if a client turns out to be overly demanding or frustrating to deal with, you'll have the power to fire them.

As a virtual assistant, having a personality that focuses on the needs of other people, with a willingness to support your clients in a variety of ways (including emotionally) is essential. Your clients will likely rely on you not just to handle the tasks assigned to you, but also to become instrumental in the operation of their business. Your goal as a VA is often to develop long-term business relationships with your clients where they trust you, seek your advice, rely on your guidance and hard work, and depend on you for their own ongoing success. You will want to choose those relationships carefully—you're in it for the long run.

Additional Startup Considerations

After establishing your business as a legal entity, one of your first responsibilities should be to acquire or compose a personalized employment contract that clearly outlines your relationship between you and your clients. Initially you can customize a boilerplate contract that you download from the internet, write your own contract from scratch, or hire a lawyer to compose the contract for you.

Having your clients sign a clear, comprehensive contract during the onboarding process will help you avoid misunderstandings later and allow you to set your boundaries. In Chapter 7, you'll see some sample contracts and learn tips for creating contracts from several successful and well-established VAs.

Choose Your Niche

Another important step in the establishment of your VA business is to determine your niche and the types of clients you want to attract. First, define your skill set and the tasks you're willing and able to perform for your clients. Keep in mind that you must be able to demonstrate your proficiency and experience using those skills and catering to the type(s) of clients you're interested in working for.

tip ⓘ

Wonder Legal USA (www.wonder.legal/us/) is just one company offering contract templates online for virtual assistants. The Virtual Assistant Assistant website (virtualassistantassistant.com) also provides contract-related templates and advice. We have included some advice and sample contracts between a virtual assistant and client in Chapter 7 as well.

Compose Your Company's Mission Statement

Once you've decided on your niche, compose a short *mission statement* for your business. A mission statement can be just one or two paragraphs long, but it should be written down and clearly define the overall objective of your business, what type(s) of services you offer, the types of clients you plan to cater to, and your overall business/customer service philosophy.

Consider including your "elevator pitch," which is a one- or two-sentence synopsis you can use to quickly describe your business and its services to someone like a potential client. Your mission statement can also include your company slogan and your ultimate goal for the business, which might be to provide VA services on a part-time or full-time basis.

To develop an effective mission statement, answer these seven questions, and then summarize your answers into a few sentences, using 200 words or less:

1. What services will you offer to your clients?
2. Within what geographical area, if any, will you operate? As a virtual assistant, you can theoretically work from anywhere, but some clients may want to set up periodic in-person meetings or want you to be in the same time zone as them.

3. What is the overall purpose or goal of your company?

4. What type(s) of clients will you serve?

5. Personally and in regard to your VA business, what are your strengths, weaknesses, opportunities, and threats?

6. Along with your expertise and resources, what services will your virtual assistant business primarily focus on? What's your niche?

> **tip**
>
> To help you stay on track and focused as you establish and operate your VA business, refer back to your mission statement often.

7. In terms of your operations and company ethics, what is important to you? What do you stand for and might this benefit your clients?

Your Home Office Is Your Primary Work Space

Even before you begin soliciting clients, you'll want to establish a solid foundation for your business, and that means setting up your home office (see Chapter 4) so you can work efficiently, gathering and installing all the software and mobile apps you'll need, and establishing how you'll manage the time-tracking and bookkeeping tasks that will be crucial to the success of your business.

From an equipment standpoint, you'll definitely need a computer with reliable high-speed internet access. If you'll also be working outside your home office, a notebook computer and/or tablet will be useful. You'll also benefit from a dedicated business phone line, a printer/copier/scanner combo (which can also include a fax machine), and a smartphone. Other necessary equipment will be determined by the type of work you'll be performing and your personal work habits.

▶ A Social Media Presence for Your Business Is Essential!

Create social media accounts on Facebook, LinkedIn, Twitter, Instagram, and other social media platforms for your business that are separate from your personal accounts. The platforms you should be the most active on (from a business standpoint) are whichever ones your target clients are using.

You'll likely find that having a Facebook Business Page and a LinkedIn presence will help you promote your VA business and find and solicit new clients, regardless of your industry. These services are powerful professional networking tools.

Creating Your Brand

One of your final steps is to give your business a name and establish your brand. (We'll talk more about this in Chapter 3.)

Part of your company's branding should include creating a logo, acquiring a domain name (e.g., www.YourCompanyName.com), establishing a company website, creating social media accounts for your business, and setting up email accounts related to your domain name (e.g., YourName@YourCompanyName.com).

You may also want to create letterhead, business cards, printed invoices, and maybe printed brochures (depending on how you'll be soliciting new clients), all of which should be consistent with your established brand in terms of appearance, messaging, color scheme, and overall design.

Your Time Matters

The time you spend catering to your clients and doing work for them is all billable time. However, the time you spend managing and marketing your VA business is not. Beyond these responsibilities, you have personal and family responsibilities you'll need to juggle.

Develop a clear understanding of the time requirements of your personal life. Next, think about how many hours you'll need to manage your business and how many hours you want to spend catering to your clients. Use that last number to set your business hours, which will determine when your clients will be able to contact you (and receive an instant or same-day response), and when you'll focus on completing client-related work.

Adopting a scheduling and project management app will help you manage your time better. Get into the habit of preplanning your day either first thing in the morning or at the end of the previous day. To avoid burnout, schedule breaks throughout each day, as well as time for lunch.

As you begin working with your clients, keep track of the time you spend catering to and handling specific tasks

> **tip** ⓘ
>
> One software package you'll be learning more about later in this book is called Adminja (www.getadminja.com). Designed specifically for virtual assistants, it handles client relationship management, project management, time tracking, and other essential tasks all from a single, cloud-based application that runs on PCs, Macs, tablets, and smartphones.
>
> HoneyBook (www.honeybook.com) is another comprehensive tool designed specifically to help VAs manage their business.

for each client. This needs to be accurately tracked down to the minute. For this, you'll want specialized time-tracking software or a mobile app.

Develop an Understanding of Each Client's Needs

The key to developing strong, long-lasting relationships with your clients is to understand their wants, needs, goals, and expectations. Some clients may come to you with a specific task to complete and provide extremely detailed, step-by-step directions for doing it. In this case, you'll be expected to follow those directions to the letter.

Other clients may know what they need done but have no idea what the best or most efficient way is to do it. In this case, you may need to first come up with a process for getting the task done, get that process approved, and then complete the work.

Once you develop a relationship with your client, prove your worth, and understand their business, then you might be able to share your ideas about how to improve their practices and work flow to save them time and money.

Knowing when and how much to speak up and share unsolicited advice or guidance to a client is something you'll need to determine on a case-by-case basis. When asked about the key personality traits that serve a virtual assistant well, many experts who were interviewed and are featured later in this book included "confidence" on their list. As the VA, you need to be confident in the value you offer to your clients—and confident enough to speak up when it's appropriate.

You'll also encounter clients who understand the *concept* of a VA but don't realize how you can be beneficial to them. By getting to know your clients and their businesses, you should be better able to recommend ways they could put your skills to good use.

In addition to providing potential and existing clients with a detailed listing of your skills and the tasks you can handle as a virtual assistant, there will be times when you should speak up and suggest to your clients ways they can better use your time and skills to help them achieve their objectives. (Again, this is where your confidence needs to kick in.)

Anytime you make this type of recommendation, however, be prepared to support it with details about the problems you can help the client solve, the exact ways you can save them time, and how working with you to perform specific tasks will save the client money.

A statement like "After seeing how your company operates, using me to perform X, Y, and Z will save your company [insert dollar amount] per month and, at the same time, free up at least [insert number] hours per week of your time" becomes an offer that's very hard for a client to pass up—especially if they already trust you and your work.

Compose a Business Plan

Once you've identified the services you want to offer and to whom and created a mission statement, you're ready to work on your business plan.

Though the specific content of your business plan will be unique, there's a basic format you should follow. The format ensures it will include all the issues you need to address, as well as provide lenders (and potential investors, if applicable) with a comprehensive document that's organized in a familiar way. Business plan creation software will help you properly format your plan, allowing you to focus more on its actual content.

If you do not plan to take on investors or seek out loans, you can streamline your business plan considerably. However, it should remain comprehensive enough that you can use it as a roadmap to operate and grow your business in the future.

Using text, charts, tables, and perhaps a few photographs to demonstrate key points, the main parts of your business plan should include the items shown in Figure 1–1.

Nobody likes to admit their personal or professional shortcomings. However, your business plan should identify any weaknesses as well as strengths, and more importantly describe how you plan to overcome them. For instance, if you're a great administrator but

Elements of a Business Plan

Cover Sheet	The title at the top should identify the document as a "Confidential Business Plan." Further down the page, add your business name, address, phone number, email address, and website URL. List yourself as the owner or proprietor.
Table of Contents	Start building your business plan by compiling a detailed table of contents to use as an outline. It will help you think about the nuts and bolts of planning your business and serve as a guide during the process. Expand the table of contents by adding subsections to the main sections (listed below) that identify all the key issues and topics to be covered.

FIGURE 1–1: **Elements of a Business Plan**

Elements of a Business Plan

Executive Summary	This section provides the reader with a brief synopsis of your virtual assistant business. Describe the business you intend to start (and its niche) and then list the reasons you specifically can make it succeed. Include your goals, industry analysis, operations, and startup timetable. Limit this section to one or two pages by writing approximately one paragraph for each main section of the plan.
Mission Statement	As discussed earlier, this is an important element of the business plan. It literally sets the tone, culture, and direction your business will adopt and explains how your company's goals will be achieved. This section can also be expanded to include statements about your company's vision, values, unique services, and philosophy.
Marketing Plan	Include an overview of the market and a description of your potential clients. Demonstrate that you've done your research. If you are a virtual assistant with a specialty, use an online business directory to compile a list of prospective clients who could use your services. Identify the competition in your niche and explain how you plan to corner the market. Discuss the advantages and drawbacks of your geographic location (if applicable), how you will deal with growth, and your strategy to promote your business through paid advertising (online and in the real world) and through other marketing and promotional efforts (including your website and social media). We'll cover this in Chapter 6.

FIGURE 1–1: **Elements of a Business Plan,** continued

Elements of a Business Plan

Organizational Plan	In this section, specify your legal structure—sole proprietorship, partnership, LLC, or corporation. Discuss your staffing needs and how you expect to meet them. Are you going to have any employees (full time or part time) or work with other virtual assistants? Are they family members, or will you go through a formal hiring process? Identify any consultants and advisors who will be assisting you, and any certifications, licenses, permits, and other regulatory issues that will affect your company's operations.
	Specify scheduled operating hours, including holidays. Provide short-term objectives for the immediate future, as well as long-range goals for the next two, three, and five years.
Management Plan	This is where you need to prove you are up to the task of operating your own business. At least initially, you'll likely be running a one-person operation from your home, but that's no problem if you are capable of successfully juggling multiple responsibilities at once. Highlight your skills and business experience. If you have prior experience handling the tasks you plan to perform for your client(s)—even as an amateur—be sure to describe it, along with any awards, credentials, accreditations, certifications, and/or other special acknowledgments you have earned.

FIGURE 1–1: **Elements of a Business Plan,** continued

Elements of a Business Plan

Financial Plan	This is where you show the source(s) of your startup capital and how you're going to use the money. If you plan to seek out investors or loans, include detailed financial statements, such as a balance sheet, P&L statement, break-even analysis, personal financial statements, and personal federal income tax returns. Take your financial data and project it out for the upcoming year to show how your business will likely do. Include a projected income statement for the second year with quarterly estimates, and then provide annual projections for three, four, and five years. Follow the same formula for cash-flow statements, along with worst-case income and cash-flow statements to show what you'll do if your plan doesn't work. You may want to work with an accountant to help compile this information.
Summary	Bring your plan together in this section in a positive and forward-thinking way.
Appendixes	Use this for supporting documents, such as your personal resume, personal and business references, and credit references. Any documentation that helps prove the validity of the information included earlier in the business plan should also be added here.

FIGURE 1-1: **Elements of a Business Plan,** continued

your written communication skills are lacking, discuss how you plan to remedy this shortcoming.

When you think your business plan is complete, take another look at it with a fresh eye. Is it a true and honest representation of the facts? Is it realistic? Does it consider all the possible variables that could affect your operation? After you're satisfied, show the plan to two or three professional associates or mentors whose input you value and trust. Ask them to be brutally honest in their evaluation. You need to know if there are any glaring problems with your plan so you can correct them before they cost you time and money.

Get Ready to Take Control!

As the owner of a virtual assistant business, get ready to take control of your professional life and make decisions that will have a direct impact on your income, happiness, schedule, and future. You get to be in charge—and you'll take the blame when and if something goes wrong.

If you have the skill set and personality to succeed as a virtual assistant, once your business is established, you'll be able to enjoy freedom, benefits, and steady income while working from home. This is a career path that offers limitless potential.

Above and beyond the responsibilities associated with establishing and running your business, you'll need to handle the tasks assigned to you by your clients. We'll talk more about what will be required of you on a day-to-day basis in the following chapter.

> **tip** ⓘ
>
> Update your business plan every year. Choose an annual date when you will sit down with your plan, compare how closely your actual operation and results followed your forecasts, and decide if your plans for the coming year need adjusting. You will also need to extend your financial forecasts out for another year, based on current and expected market conditions.

Potential Responsibilities of a Virtual Assistant

Pursuing the role of a virtual assistant as a career path involves two distinct areas of responsibility. First, you need to establish and manage your business. Second, you need to define your niche and then successfully complete all the tasks assigned to you by your clients.

The first set of responsibilities is consistent for all virtual assistants who opt to work for themselves (as opposed to working for an agency). The second set of responsibilities will vary greatly, depending on your skill set, your experience, the clients you cater to, the industries your clients work in, and the specific needs of those clients.

Why Business Leaders and Companies Should Hire Virtual Assistants

To you, the question of why someone should hire you as a virtual assistant might seem like a no-brainer. However, chances are your potential clients will need a bit of convincing. Consider questions, concerns, and objections from their point of view.

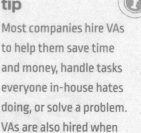

tip

Most companies hire VAs to help them save time and money, handle tasks everyone in-house hates doing, or solve a problem. VAs are also hired when nobody in-house has the skill set needed to accomplish a specific task, and it's more cost-effective to outsource that work. Keep this in mind as you're establishing and branding your VA business and then begin soliciting clients.

tip

As a startup virtual assistant, the more specific you are when creating your services menu and deciding which types of clients you want to target, the easier it'll be for you to market yourself to potential clients and then charge the highest rates possible, because you know you'll be providing the services and solutions those clients require.

It's important that you can clearly identify what your clients need. How can you save your clients time and/ or money? What existing problems can you solve for your clients?

Yes, many small business owners, corporate executives, startups, business consultants, and entrepreneurs could benefit from hiring one or more VAs to help ease their workload. Once you make a potential client aware that they might need you, be prepared to quickly follow up with specifics.

Where VAs really show their worth is stepping in to handle time-consuming and repetitive tasks that keep their clients from doing the work that makes them the most money or allows them to accomplish their primary goals. If someone is spending several hours per day managing their email inbox and schedule (or dealing with their bookkeeping, website, or social media presence), they could delegate those tasks to a VA and save themselves 10 or 20 hours per week. Suddenly the concept of working with a VA becomes very attractive.

Many business leaders also have a list of jobs that they hate doing and that they avoid, so those responsibilities don't get handled properly. These are other tasks a VA could typically take on. Depending on your chosen niche as a VA, it's your job to help a client quickly identify their biggest time wasters and demonstrate how you can handle those tasks in a cost-effective way.

From a marketing standpoint, you need to show them not only how you can be a problem solver and time-saver, but also that hiring a VA is not too expensive (a common misconception). By taking over unprofitable tasks, you're allowing them to earn more money, grow their business, better cater to their own customers/clients, and free up their own time.

By hiring virtual assistants, a company is delegating tasks to an independent contractor who is paid a flat fee. They are not responsible for providing benefits, an office, training, or equipment, but they can use VAs to handle tasks that are instrumental to the operation, productivity, and growth of their business.

Always consider things from a potential client's perspective. Learn as much as you can about them in advance, and then tailor your services menu, expertise, and experience to meet their immediate needs.

Simply by visiting a company's website, doing an internet search on them (via Google or Bing), and looking them up on social media (such as LinkedIn, Facebook, and Twitter), you can learn a lot very quickly. Use that knowledge to help sell yourself and your services to potential clients by demonstrating that you understand their business, industry, and needs.

Define Your Niche as a VA

Some virtual assistants come from a corporate background or held a full-time job in a specific field and choose to use those skills to complete similar tasks for their clients. It's not uncommon, however, for people breaking into the VA field to first obtain training to expand their skill set. As you're thinking about which services you may want to offer clients, consider:

▶ The industries you're truly interested in
▶ Specific tasks you enjoy doing
▶ The activities you're good at

warning

When selecting your niche as a virtual assistant and compiling the menu of services you plan to offer, do not choose based solely on what you think is in high demand. Select your niche based on your passion, skill set, and experience, so that you'll truly be able to enjoy your work—not just be good at it. If you love what you're doing, you'll be more dedicated, work harder, and avoid burnout. Your clients will also notice and appreciate your passion.

▶ The marketable work experience you already have that will give you credibility with potential clients

Next, consider how you'll tap your existing interests and skill set when deciding which services you'll offer to clients and the types of clients you're best suited to work with. Use the worksheet on page 21 to help you determine what you could offer to potential clients.

Ultimately, once you establish your business, niche, and brand, and then begin promoting your virtual assistant business, potential clients will want to know:

▶ *Exactly what you offer*. This includes your menu of available services and the level of attention a client will receive. How do you differentiate yourself from the vast pool of generalists vying for their business?

▶ *Whether or not what you're offering is a good fit*. The client will need to determine quickly if you can help them save time, save money, or solve the problem(s) they're currently facing.

▶ *How much it will cost*. Can the client justify the expense of hiring you vs. hiring someone else or handling the work in-house?

The faster you can convey this information to potential clients online (through email, social media, or your website), on the phone, or in person (at a professional networking event, for example), the easier it'll be for you to land clients.

After choosing a niche (or specialty), do some research online to determine who your competition will be, whether there's a market for what you plan to offer, and specifically who your potential clients might be. Create a list of at least 10 to 15 individuals or companies that might want to hire you and that you'd want to work for.

Only after you know what you want to offer and who you want to offer it to, and after you've determined there's a need for your services, should you decide to pursue that niche and brand your virtual assistant business accordingly.

Use the worksheet in Figure 2–1 on page 21 to help you determine what services you'll offer to clients and

> **tip** ⓘ
>
> Ask yourself: Are your target clients already familiar with the concept of a virtual assistant, or will you need to educate them on what a VA is and does before you sell them on your services and qualifications? If potential clients don't even know what a virtual assistant is, persuading them to hire you will pose a much bigger challenge. At least initially, try to seek out potential clients who already know and understand the benefits of working with virtual assistants.

then narrow down the type(s) of clients you'd like to work with as a virtual assistant. Be honest with yourself about who you are and what you're capable of, and then research online to determine exactly how your skill set and experience could be put to proper use.

Creating Your Niche Worksheet

Based on your existing skill set and interests, what five industries are you most interested in working in, or what type(s) of clients are you best suited to cater to?

1. _____

2. _____

3. _____

4. _____

5. _____

What are three related industries (or types of businesses) that also require the services you plan to offer?

1. _____

2. _____

3. _____

Based on your existing skill set, list five tasks/services you could begin providing immediately to your clients.

1. _____

2. _____

3. _____

4. _____

5. _____

FIGURE 2–1: **Creating Your Niche Worksheet**

Creating Your Niche Worksheet

Starting with the term *virtual assistant*, create a list of at least ten keywords* or search phrases related to your niche that a potential client might use to find you online.

1. _____
2. _____
3. _____
4. _____
5. _____
6. _____
7. _____
8. _____
9. _____
10. _____

*Consider using a free online keyword selection tool to help compile this list. Popular keyword selection tools include:

- Google Ads Keyword Planner: https://ads.google.com/home/tools/keyword-planner
- Keyword Tool: https://keywordtool.io
- KWFinder: https://kwfinder.com
- WordStream: https://www.wordstream.com/keywords
- Wordtracker: https://www.wordtracker.com/

What tasks or services do you really enjoy doing, are good at, and have proven experience completing successfully?

1. _____
2. _____
3. _____
4. _____
5. _____

FIGURE 2–1: **Creating Your Niche Worksheet,** continued

Creating Your Niche Worksheet

What type(s) of potential clients currently need people with your skill set and interests?

_____

_____

_____

Through past work experience, completed training/education, and/or certifications, how can you prove to a potential client that you can successfully handle the services you plan to offer?

_____

_____

_____

What five tasks do you truly hate doing, or what tasks might you be asked to complete by clients that you're not qualified to handle? (Keep in mind, if you wind up spending too much time doing tasks you dislike, it could cause you to burn out quickly. Likewise, if you take on tasks that you're not capable of handling, this could cause tremendous frustration for you and the client and lead to costly mistakes.)

1. _____

2. _____

3. _____

4. _____

5. _____

Based on your area(s) of interest, what additional training do you still need to properly handle the tasks clients may hire you to handle? What's your plan for obtaining the necessary training or expanding your skill set accordingly?

_____

_____

_____

FIGURE 2–1: **Creating Your Niche Worksheet,** continued

Creating Your Niche Worksheet

Using as much detail as possible, describe your ideal client(s) and what you'll do for them.

_____

_____

_____

How will you set yourself apart from competing VAs and justify the rates you plan to charge your clients?

_____

_____

_____

FIGURE 2–1: **Creating Your Niche Worksheet,** continued

Start Compiling Your Services Menu

There is no set list of services that a virtual assistant can or should offer. The services you provide are dictated by your skill set and experience, along with what your clients demand. That said, below are some typical tasks VAs handle for their clients.

General Administrative Tasks

The price a VA can charge for these more generalized services is anywhere from $15 to $25 per hour. The main qualification for this type of work is previous experience as an office assistant, personal assistant, administrative assistant, or executive assistant.

General administrative tasks a VA might be hired to handle include:

▶ Answering and directing phone calls
▶ Coordinating meetings
▶ Customer service (entry-level)
▶ Data entry
▶ Dictation and transcription
▶ Expenses and invoicing

- ▶ File management
- ▶ Identifying business leads
- ▶ Inbox management (email)
- ▶ Making reservations related to client dining
- ▶ Making travel arrangements
- ▶ Organizing schedules and calendars
- ▶ Outbound telemarketing/sales
- ▶ Research
- ▶ Scheduling appointments and calendar management
- ▶ Sending gifts

> **tip** ⓘ
>
> Some VAs specialize exclusively in managing their clients' email inboxes, handling their schedules or calendars, or receiving incoming calls on their behalf. Having a specialty makes you more appealing to clients with specific needs.

Specialized Tasks

For someone with more specialized skills, a higher level of education, a certification in a particular field, or extensive corporate experience, you could charge anywhere from $25 to $100 per hour for your work (and sometimes more).

The more specialized the service you provide and the more skill it requires, the more you can charge. Here are some examples:

- ▶ Blog writing, article writing, copywriting, or podcast writing/production
- ▶ Bookkeeping
- ▶ Computer and online security
- ▶ Email marketing and email list opt-in/opt-out management
- ▶ Event planning
- ▶ Grant or proposal writing
- ▶ Graphic design and illustration
- ▶ Invoice creation/accounts receivable/billing
- ▶ Language translation services
- ▶ Managing aspects of an ecommerce website (e.g., customer service, tracking orders, invoicing, shipping, dealing with returns/exchanges, tracking inventory, etc.)
- ▶ Meeting planning
- ▶ Online advertising and marketing (SEO)
- ▶ Payroll
- ▶ Photography and photo editing
- ▶ Programming
- ▶ Public relations (e.g., writing and distributing press releases, contacting the media, sending out products for review, booking media interviews, etc.)

▶ Sales enrichment and qualification

▶ Social media account management

▶ Speech writing or PowerPoint design

▶ Spreadsheet and/or database design and management

▶ Talent sourcing and qualification (HR-related tasks)

▶ Video production and/or editing for YouTube or other online presence

▶ Website content creation

▶ Website design and updating

▶ Word processing and editing/proofreading

> **tip**
>
> If as a VA you cater to just one industry (which is common), your services list should specifically target and appeal to prospective clients working in that industry. If your VA business caters to multiple industries, have separate services lists categorized by industry, even if some of those services overlap.

Your Services Menu

Whether you promote your virtual assistant business online, in print, or in person, a potential client will want to know the exact services you offer, the cost of those services, your availability, and (when applicable) how quickly you can get something done.

You'll want to provide potential clients with your unique menu of services in an easy-to-read format. This services menu should be showcased on your website, but you should also send a printed copy (or a PDF file) to prospective clients upon request.

Some VAs choose to sort their services listings by industry. For example, a prospective client who clicks on the Services menu option on your site would see a submenu that lists key industries you cater to. A sample submenu might look like this: Marketing, Real Estate, Medical, Property Management, Business Consultants, Public Speakers, Contractors, Administrative Assistants, Executive Assistants, or Recruitment Assistants. Under each submenu heading, you would list the specific tasks or services you provide.

> **fun fact**
>
> If you're still having trouble compiling your services menu, check out the "Virtual Assistant Services in 2021 (The Comprehensive Guide)," published on the OkayRelax Blog (https://okayrelax.com/virtual-assistant-services-2021-comprehensive-guide), for some ideas. It includes a list of 201 services VAs can offer.

Your About Us Page

As you'll discover in Chapter 3, while your Services web page should describe the types of work you can do for your clients, your About Us page (which could also be titled "Meet [Your First Name]") should focus on your skill set, education, experience, work ethic, business philosophy, and overall qualifications. This page should make it clear to clients that you're fully capable of providing the services you're offering.

Additional key points to quickly get across on your About Us page include:

tip

Do your research. Visit the websites for at least five to ten other virtual assistants. Start with the VAs interviewed later in this book. Look at how each VA lists and then describes the services they offer. Notice how the service descriptions often explain the benefit(s) to the potential client, yet everything is written in a succinct, easy-to-understand way.

> ▶ You nicely match the potential client's requirements.
> ▶ You are college educated (if applicable).
> ▶ English is your native language (if you're based in North America and targeting English-speaking clients).
> ▶ Your hours of operation (to show that you're available during the hours the client needs you).
> ▶ You specialize in working in the same industry as the prospective client.
> ▶ What time zone you're based in.

Should You Start Your Own VA Business or Work with an Agency?

Not everyone who has what it takes to be an amazing virtual assistant has the wherewithal to start and manage their own business. If you fall into this category, or you simply don't want to deal with the day-to-day responsibilities of operating a small business, consider working for a virtual assistant agency.

Allow the agency to handle the administrative tasks of running and marketing the business, as well as finding and landing clients on your behalf. You could also receive training and have the opportunity to network with other VAs while working with an agency. While you'll have a boss, chances are you'll still enjoy a lot of flexibility in your schedule and be able to determine the types of projects you take on.

The biggest drawback to working with an agency is that the agency takes a substantial commission based on your earnings, so you'll earn less (sometimes much less) than if you work independently.

Lauren Gall, the cofounder of VaVa Virtual Assistants (https://vavavirtual.com/); Cindy Opong, the founder of Creative Assistants (https://www.creativeassistants.com/); and Latrice

Prater, founder of The Digital Solutions Team (https://www.thedigitalsolutionsteam.com/), each own and operate a virtual assistant agency that has numerous VAs working for them to service their many clients. In the following interviews with them, you'll discover what it takes to be a successful virtual assistant, as well as learn the pros and cons of working as a VA for an established agency.

Meet Lauren Gall, Cofounder of VaVa Virtual Assistants

VaVa Virtual Assistants is based in Toluca Lake, California, and was founded in 2011 by Lauren Gall and Melanie Ammerman. They have grown their agency 97 percent from one year to the next, and currently have more than 45 U.S.-based virtual assistants working for them.

How did you become a virtual assistant and why did you start your own agency?

Lauren Gall: Prior to working as a virtual assistant and launching the agency, I was working at a sales job selling virtual reception and eFax solutions for a company based in Hollywood, California. In that job, I was communicating with small business owners all day long. I discovered they all had a need for one or more virtual assistants, because they didn't have the budget to hire someone in-house, or they didn't have enough work to justify hiring a part-time or full-time employee.

I began thinking that I could start a side business as a virtual assistant. I teamed up with my cofounder, and we decided to launch the agency within a week. It took less than three months to determine that operating a virtual assistant agency was a viable business. Initially, both myself and my business partner were running the business and servicing our clients working as virtual assistants. It was about one year after starting the agency that we hired our first virtual assistant as an independent contractor.

How do you define the role of a virtual assistant?

Gall: At least in terms of what our agency offers, I define the role of a virtual assistant as a strategic partner who is outsourced. A VA is someone who will manage or complete the activities that the client does not have time to do, does not want to do, or that are repetitive tasks that waste the client's valuable time.

Having worked with so many independent VAs over the years, what would you say are the most important personality traits that someone starting out in this field must possess?

Gall: You have to be friendly, be communicative, and be an outside-of-the-box thinker. When we get clients that don't know what they want, the VA needs to partner and communicate with them to provide them with tips and ideas. A good VA needs to be able to strategize, think on their feet, and understand how to get a job done. Someone who needs a lot of hand-holding would not make a good virtual assistant.

What should a VA do to differentiate themselves from their competition?

Gall: Never stop learning and expanding your skill set. There are a lot of courses out there that you can do virtually that will provide you with new marketable skills that are in demand by your potential or existing clients. Once you have acquired new skills or experiences, highlight those in your resume or services listing.

When engaged in initial conversations with prospective clients, don't just highlight what you can do. After doing your research, explain why you want to work with that client. At the end of the day, being a good VA is simply about consistently doing good work. If you can, provide potential clients with specific examples or case studies related to what you've done in the past. Talk about the work and the results you achieved.

If you're first starting out, consider offering a prospective new client a small amount of your time for free, to demonstrate your capabilities. This will get you in the door. It's then your responsibility to provide a high level of service.

How important is it for a virtual assistant to develop a niche, as opposed to being a generalist in the services they offer?

Gall: Our agency is more generalized. We do not cater to a specific industry or type of client. For someone starting out on their own, however, it's good to have a niche, because it will help to set you apart. Even if you have a niche, don't close your door to potential opportunities. It's always good to gain new experiences whenever it makes sense for your business.

How important is it for a virtual assistant to brand themselves and their business?

Gall: It's very important. It's also very important to be consistent with your branding. Strive to become a thought leader in your industry.

For a virtual assistant who ventures off on their own and chooses not to work with an agency, what advice can you offer about how to find and land new clients?

Gall: Make connections in the industry and tell as many people as you can about what you do. There are a lot of online-based groups, especially on Facebook, composed of individuals and companies that are looking to hire a virtual assistant. Become active within those online groups and provide them with your value. Offer advice and share your knowledge without taking a hard-sell approach. If you demonstrate that you're knowledgeable and capable, potential clients who meet you online will eventually come to you and hire you.

As you create leads for your pipeline, even if they don't hire you right away, follow up with them periodically. Another thing I recommend to virtual assistants who are first starting out is to find yourself a mentor who is a well-established VA. One of the benefits to working for an agency is that you automatically have mentors at your disposal. When I first started out as a virtual assistant, one of the ways I landed my first few clients was through referrals from my mentor, who could not take on the additional work herself.

Once you land your first few clients and you consistently do good work for them, your name will spread like wildfire and you'll often receive referrals from those clients.

Independent virtual assistants are often forced to charge higher rates than large agencies or other VAs working outside the United States. When a prospective client says "I can find someone to do this same work for much less money," how would you respond?

Gall: Many companies and individuals who are based in the United States have discovered that working with someone based in another time zone can be challenging from a scheduling standpoint, and that working with someone who does not natively speak the same language can easily cause miscommunications and mistakes. When a VA is working in a time zone that has a 3-, 6-, or 12-hour difference, this makes it difficult for the client to hold virtual meetings or phone calls with their VA, or to meet tight deadlines. Our experience with potential clients who have hired VAs for less is that they come back to us later with the realization that you get what you pay for. Those VAs didn't offer as much value.

Do you have advice for a VA who encounters a difficult or overly demanding client?

Gall: One benefit to working for an agency is that the agency deals with client-related issues that come up. I would say that if you're the one who is marketing your business to prospective clients, during your initial interactions with that person, you should be able to get a good idea about whether they'll be a good fit for you. If you don't think a prospective client will be a good match, be polite, but turn down the work.

Right at the start, set clear boundaries with a client and define what you expect from them in terms of the relationship. These should also be outlined in your contract. A difficult client can come in many forms. For example, it could be someone who does not respect your working hours and tries to contact you in the middle of the night to work on a task, and then gets annoyed when you're not available. A difficult client might also be someone who does not communicate clearly, which leads to misunderstandings, or who consistently pays their outstanding invoices 20 or more days late.

I recommend overcommunicating and be very clear about what you, as the VA, need from the relationship. Instead of wasting too much time dealing with the difficult clients, be prepared to let them go if you can't resolve the issues in a quick and professional way.

A virtual assistant agency will provide the written contract between the client and the VA subcontracted to work with that client. What advice can you offer for someone who needs to create their own contract?

Gall: I would have a contract custom written. If you use a boilerplate contract, be prepared to edit it heavily before you present it to a client during the onboarding process. Also understand that your contract will likely need to be edited over time. I suggest having a lawyer write up the actual document once you determine what it needs to include. Make sure the contract outlines what services you'll provide, your cancelation policy, your payment policy, and your hours of operation. If something important is not included within your contract, understand that you will have clients who will try to take advantage of you.

Why should a VA who is first starting out team up with an agency?

Gall: Working with an agency is definitely something I recommend. All you need to do as the VA is consistently provide good work. The agency will match you up with clients, set your rates, handle billing, and manage the client relationship. The agency will also often provide training and help you gain real-world experience working as a virtual assistant. When you work for an agency, you're still working from home, but you have a team available to support you, learn from, and communicate with every single day.

The hourly rate we can charge for hiring our VAs is based on their experience. At our agency, this ranges from $15 to $30 per hour for the services we offer to our clients. The agency then typically earns a 50 percent commission, which is paid out of the VA's earnings. This, however, varies by client.

When a virtual assistant is seeking out an agency to work with, what should they look for?

Gall: Look at the agency's culture and values, as well as how long they've been in operation. Also determine what the agency does for its team members in terms of ongoing training, team building, and engagement. Do research about the agency in advance and understand what services the agency provides to what types of clients. Look for an agency that would be a good fit for you, based on your qualifications.

A virtual assistant agency is a very technology-based business. If you come to us for an interview and you can't figure out how to join a Zoom video call, this is a huge red flag for us. We also look at your communication skills and will evaluate your cover letter, for example. It should contain zero errors. Ultimately, a virtual assistant should feel like they're well-connected with the agency they choose to work with.

Do you have any other advice for up-and-coming virtual assistants?

Gall: Again, find yourself a mentor. Even if you're not actually working for or with your mentor, find someone you can meet with once or twice a month, and whom you can learn from and share ideas with. Choose a mentor you can lean on, especially if you don't have a business partner. If you're running a VA business on your own, there will be times when you need to make important decisions. Having someone whose opinion you trust and value will make it easier to make those crucial decisions.

As a VA, you're going to make mistakes. When this happens, learn from your mistakes, and do everything possible to never repeat them. Moving forward, the real challenges kick in when you have your client roster entirely filled, and you need to manage all their needs and, at the same time, manage and run your own business.

Also become good at professional networking, both online and in the real world. This is likely how you'll find most of your clients.

Meet Cindy Opong, Founder of Creative Assistants

Cindy Opong started working as a virtual assistant in 2002. Her agency, Creative Assistants, currently has a team of six VAs working for her to support more than a dozen clients. They specialize in catering to the needs of entrepreneurs and small businesses across a variety of sectors, including corporate consultants, professional speakers, authors, and nonprofits.

In the past, Opong served as president of the International Virtual Assistants Association (IVAA), a not-for-profit professional trade association composed of independent business owners who provide virtual administrative, creative, and/or technical services to a wide array of clientele while working remotely.

Why did you originally become a VA and decide to establish Creative Assistants?

Cindy Opong: I came from the corporate world. I was working as an executive assistant at Hewlett-Packard and got caught in the layoffs that happened within the tech industry back in the early 2000s. I always had the desire to have my own business, and after being laid off, it seemed like the ideal time for me to start one. At that time in my life, I was looking for a job that offered flexibility and that would allow me to do some traveling. In 2002, I came across some information about virtual assistants and discovered it was exactly the type of work I was looking for.

Back in 2002, a virtual assistant's responsibilities were very different. The work was very much like that of a traditional administrative assistant. At first, I had to learn a lot on my own. I eventually found some mentors and became active in a professional association.

Almost 20 years later, I have six VAs working under me that I call on for general services, and a handful of others I use when I need more specialized services handled for my business or my clients.

How do you define the role of a virtual assistant?

Opong: My role as a virtual assistant, and the role of the VAs working for me, is to support and run the back end of a client's business so they can focus more on what they're really good at. My agency focuses on back-end office management for consultants. These are people who were once very high up in the corporate world, and who now work full time as business consultants. These people were used to having an executive assistant, and I take on that role for them.

In your opinion, what are the key personality traits that a virtual assistant needs to be successful?

Opong: A virtual assistant needs to be dedicated and consider this to be a long-term career opportunity. They need to have a business mindset. A VA also needs to be resourceful. When a client says "I need X, Y, and Z," it's up to the VA to figure out how to make that happen and to know what tools they should use.

For someone interested in becoming a virtual assistant, do you think they should start off by working for an agency?

Opong: I think it's very helpful to first become a subcontractor working for another virtual assistant or an agency. This will provide the mentoring you need and the ability to learn how things work, allow you to gain experience, and ultimately get recommendations, which you can use to land your own clients. As an agency, we assign very specific client tasks to the VAs we work with, based on that VA's skill set and experience.

When you first begin speaking with a virtual assistant who is interested in working for your agency, what do you look for in that applicant?

Opong: I am looking for somebody with some experience and who has thought through their career path. They have a plan for themselves and what they're trying to accomplish. I don't want to waste time having a new VA come onboard, have them work for a month or so, and then have them decide the work or pay isn't for them, so they leave. I am looking for people with specific skill sets. For my agency, we look for people who are already proficient using Google Workspace and Microsoft Office, for example. I look for applicants who can discuss these tools off the top of their head and explain to me exactly how they'd be used to accomplish specific tasks.

For someone who chooses to work independently as a virtual assistant, what advice can you share about finding and landing those first few clients?

Opong: Learn how to network and focus on those activities. There is a lot of in-person and local networking that can be done in the real world, as well as plenty of networking opportunities using the internet and social media. Get out there with the goal of getting your name known. Figure out the Facebook groups, LinkedIn Groups, and associations where your target clients may be hanging out and become active there.

Volunteer with professional organizations and associations related to the industries you want to work in as a virtual assistant. As a volunteer, people will get to see you at work. If you impress them and they discover you're a virtual assistant, they're more apt to seek out your services when they're needed. Also reach out to people you know from your past work life, for example, and ask for referrals. Let people know what you're now doing as a virtual assistant and what types of services you offer.

One key to success for most VAs is to build long-term relationships with clients. What advice can you share for how to do this?

Opong: Always go above and beyond when working on projects for your clients and demonstrate your reliability and dedication. Also be sure to vet your clients carefully. Keep in mind, there are many companies and individuals who want to hire a VA to handle a single, one-time project, and they're not looking for a long-term relationship. Look for clients that have the right level of income to be able to work with you on a consistent basis. As you're interviewing a prospective client, ask about their budget. If they're only looking to pay $10 per hour for a VA, that might not be a good fit, but a client that can afford at least $1,000 per month may be a more viable client for you.

Now that you're a successful and experienced virtual assistant, if you were starting from scratch today to launch your business, what would you do differently?

Opong: I would immediately get involved with some training programs and professional associations. I would also focus my energies on networking to find new clients

fun fact ☺

Freelance University (www.freelanceu.com/) offers online training designed to help virtual assistants and other freelancers develop the right skills and confidence to build thriving businesses. Since it was founded in 2008, more than 20,000 students have graduated from the program. Once registered, students have access to more than 80 courses covering 10 specialized training tasks related to founding and operating a successful virtual assistant business.

and create a business plan and marketing plan right at the start. One excellent training program that I highly recommend for VAs is called Freelance University. Choose a training program that caters specifically to the virtual assistant industry.

As a result of constantly evolving technologies and online collaboration tools, as well as how business operations have changed because of the COVID-19 pandemic, how do you see the role of a virtual assistant changing over the next three to five years?

Opong: I think the need for virtual assistants will be increasing dramatically. I believe the COVID-19 pandemic has opened the eyes of business operators, who now realize the need and benefits of working with a virtual assistant and can see this as a viable option.

What are the biggest mistakes you see virtual assistants make, and how can someone avoid those mistakes?

Opong: Communications is a key part of being a successful virtual assistant. Really work on enhancing your written and verbal communication skills, especially when it comes to using digital technologies, such as email, voice calls, video calls, virtual meetings, and online collaboration tools. If you make a mistake, own up to it, and then be willing to fix it on your own dime.

Another suggestion I can make is to avoid sticking with a client that you know is not a good fit for you. What I have learned over the years is that if you let go of a bad client, a new and better client will almost always come along relatively quickly.

Meet Latrice Prater, Founder of The Digital Solutions Team

Based near Austin, Texas, The Digital Solutions Team is a virtual assistant agency that provides administrative, technical, and launch support services exclusively to female business owners and entrepreneurs. Under the leadership of Latrice Prater, in a little over a year, the boutique agency has grown to employ a team of more than five virtual assistants. Before founding Digital Solutions, Prater worked in the corporate world as a full-time administrative and then executive assistant.

How did you get started as a virtual assistant and what made you found The Digital Solutions Team?

Latrice Prater: I got my bachelor's degree in child development and my master's degree in education, because originally I wanted to be a teacher. However, I ultimately decided that I did not want to be confined to a classroom. Over the years, I have worked as a teacher, as a customer service representative, for a juvenile detention facility, and for the IRS. I also became a licensed life insurance agent, a life coach, and an ordained minister as a side job so I could officiate weddings. Toward the later part of my professional life, I served as an executive assistant for a medical company in San Diego, starting in 2016.

As an executive assistant, I discovered I had a knack for organization and multitasking. Until then, no job was able to hold my attention. I always had an itch to become an entrepreneur and start my own business. I did, however, make money in all my different career paths and business ventures. When I learned about what a virtual assistant was via the Upwork.com website, I decided to give that a try to earn some extra money.

On Upwork.com (www.upwork.com), I listed myself as a virtual administrative assistant to see how it would go. I wound up landing a few clients. This success made me think that becoming a virtual assistant could become a lucrative full-time career opportunity. I did a bunch of research, and then in the beginning of 2020, I decided to give it a try. I was tired of working as an employee for a company that made me feel undervalued and underappreciated. I also did not want to have to beg a superior if I wanted a day off.

I loved being a behind-the-scenes support person and knew that I could handle these responsibilities for clients by working from home as a part-time virtual assistant. I literally built my own website and began to market myself as a virtual assistant on Facebook and LinkedIn. As a mother of three kids, I knew a plan was needed and that I could not just quit my lucrative full-time corporate job. I juggled my corporate job and my VA job for a bit until I knew that the VA business would offer enough income to replace my full-time job. That's how it all started.

In the beginning of February 2020, just before COVID-19 got real, I quit my full-time job and launched my virtual assistant business on a full-time basis. By the end of February 2020, I was earning the same amount as an independent VA as I was in my executive assistant job.

How do the responsibilities of an administrative assistant or executive assistant working in corporate America differ from being an independent virtual assistant?

Prater: Honestly, the biggest difference is the mindset. The actual tasks and responsibilities are very similar. It all depends on the clients you work with. When I am discussing what I do with prospective clients, I simply explain that the only difference between my work as an experienced executive assistant and as a VA is that I now work virtually from my home for a handful of clients. The required skill set is the same.

I describe my role as a VA as someone who handles the tasks of a high-level executive assistant, team leader, or online business manager. I describe my role as a partner in each of my clients' businesses. I am an integrator, fixer, and facilitator who pays attention to all the small details. I anticipate what could go wrong, and I try to be two steps ahead so I can fix the situation quickly. I also describe myself as a coach because my clients come to me when they're stuck on something. I become a sounding board for new ideas.

Many of my clients are not looking for a VA who sits around waiting for tasks to be assigned. They're looking for someone who is proactive, who wants to help their clients grow and scale. As a VA, I need to understand the business I am working with. I want someone's experience working with me to be transformational. My role often goes well beyond just the admin stuff that an executive assistant might handle.

How do you learn as much as possible about your clients so that you can offer that higher level of contribution and become a valued resource?

Prater: I do a lot of research about the companies I will be working for. I do a deep dive online and rely on social media to learn about each company and the people I will be working with at that company. I also ask a lot of questions during the discovery call and when onboarding a new client. I try to determine what challenges a client is facing and figure out all of the ways I can help the business achieve its objectives.

What do you believe are the most important personality traits a virtual assistant must have to succeed?

Prater: I would say the most important trait is being proactive and not afraid to talk to people. Now that I have begun hiring VAs for my agency, I have discovered that many of the applicants are introverted and very quiet. Many VAs also lack initiative and refuse to do the extra work needed to determine what more they can do for a client. Many VAs are only willing to do the bare minimum, and I think that's wrong.

When I am hiring a new VA to work with my agency, I have a three-round process that includes two separate written applications and then an in-depth interview. In the first round, I try to determine what skills the applicant is proficient in, and I administer some personality testing as well. These tests help me determine what makes an applicant tick. I need to know how much training a VA will need before they can start generating income. Right now, I will only consider working with VAs based in the United States, because that's where I and all my clients are located.

I need VAs who know how to talk to people and know how to work as a team, but also know how to work independently. This information typically comes from the interview. I look for people who know how to take charge, because as a VA, it's sometimes necessary to reel in a client so they don't go off on tangents. I also look for people who are proactive and who take the initiative when they're working. During the second round of the application process, I create realistic scenarios related to client management, for example, and ask the applicant how they'd respond to those situations. I am also looking for VAs who can just be themselves and who are not afraid to do that.

What are the biggest mistakes you've seen virtual assistants make?

Prater: I have seen independent VAs accept work at a rate that was too low and that they knew going in would not allow them to support themselves. I also have seen VAs working with clients who were overly demanding and who constantly tried to take advantage of them. Virtual assistants need to be careful of the clients they take on and develop an understanding of what they're getting into before they commit themselves to a no-win situation. Create standards, boundaries, and limits, and then stick to them, while understanding some flexibility will be necessary from time to time.

Also, instead of focusing on building a solid business structure, I have seen VAs seeking out costly and time-consuming certifications that they simply don't need. Make sure you invest your time and money into the right things.

If you're in charge of creating and managing your client's calendar and schedule, it's your responsibility to build buffers into a client's day so they can take breaks and eat lunch, for example. When I know a client is too busy, I will block in a lunch break for them. For both a virtual assistant and a client, self-care is essential.

In your opinion, what is the best and worst thing about working as a virtual assistant?

Prater: For me, the best thing is the relationships that I get to build doing this. I have met a lot of great people. The worst thing is not always setting boundaries and then having to deal with and overcome personal burnout. In conclusion, I'd tell people to show up, do the work, and be yourself, so you can attract the types of clients you want to attract. When you do this, the money will follow.

Establish a Strong Foundation for Your Virtual Assistant Business

If you decide to operate your own VA business, you already know you need to create a niche for yourself and cultivate the appropriate skill set to meet your clients' needs. But when it comes to creating a strong foundation for your business, you want to focus on defining and establishing its brand. That's what we'll be talking about in the next chapter.

Branding Your Virtual Assistant Business

Once you know what you want to do as a virtual assistant and the type(s) of clients you're interested in working with, it's important to create a brand for your business that will appeal to those clients. When making the creative decisions around developing your brand, put yourself in the shoes of your prospective clients and consider what would catch their attention.

There are many aspects to a company's brand, both in the real world and online. It's essential that all elements of your brand work together in a synergistic way from a messaging, perception, and visual standpoint. As an independent business operator, you should make sure your brand conveys a professional image. While there's room for creativity and cleverness, remember that you want to be taken seriously by prospective clients.

fun fact

Over time, as your virtual assistant business grows and evolves, it may be necessary to rebrand or alter your branding to give it a broader appeal or to convey additional information about the services your company offers.

Elements of a Company's Brand

Developing your brand starts with brainstorming the perfect name for your company. From there, you'll want to build your brand based on who you want to appeal to and what you're trying to accomplish.

Every element of your brand should help establish your company as easily recognizable, memorable, professional, experienced, and reputable. While each element should stand out on its own, they should all work seamlessly together as well. For example, you should use the same font(s), color scheme, imagery, and core design elements throughout, as appropriate.

Let's explore many of the key elements that work together to make up a company's brand.

The Company Name

Your company's name can say a lot about who you are and what you do. If you're working alone in your VA business, you might consider including your own name in the company name (e.g., "Jane the Virtual Assistant" or "Virtual Office Administration by Jane"). However, if you're planning to grow over time, this could make your business look too small.

warning

Before settling on a company name, make sure the [name].com website URL is available for that name. Also double-check that there's nothing potentially offensive about your chosen name.

When brainstorming your company name, look for something that's memorable, easy to spell, meaningful, not too long, and unique. Your name should not be easily confused with another business (especially another virtual assistant business), nor should it violate another company's intellectual property (such as their copyright or trademark).

Coming up with the perfect company name will take some brainstorming, research, and time. Don't just settle for the first thing that pops into your head. Develop a list of at least ten potential company names or variations, and ask friends, relatives, colleagues, and even potential clients for their opinion.

If you start repeatedly hearing the same objections to a potential name, remove it from your list. Ultimately, the name you choose will represent your business for as long as it exists. Avoid a name that taps into a current trend. It should have evergreen appeal and be something that you, as the business owner, absolutely love. It should also be something that will appeal to your intended clients.

Begin your brainstorming session by coming up with a list of at least 12 keywords associated with your business (starting with *virtual*). Pick descriptive words associated not just with being a virtual assistant, but also with the services you plan to provide to your clients, such as *bookkeeping, word processing, scheduling, website design, receptionist,* or *executive* assistant. Use Figure 3–1 on page 42 to help you figure this out.

Also consider keywords related to your location and words that describe how you conduct business (i.e., your company's core values), like *affordable, dedicated, expert, experienced,* or *honest*. You may find a thesaurus helpful in compiling this master keyword list.

tip ⓘ

Once you know what primary industry your potential clients will be working in and have identified the types of services you'll be offering, consider incorporating these ideas into your company name. For example, "Boston Virtual Bookkeepers" explains exactly what you do and where you're based. To a potential client looking for a VA who specializes in bookkeeping and who is located in their time zone, this company name conveys exactly the right information.

A Mission Statement and Slogan

Back in Chapter 1, you were encouraged to compose a detailed mission statement that described your business philosophy and objectives. Based on the company name and mission statement you've chosen for your virtual assistant business, now it's time to come up with a company slogan.

According to B12, a company that builds websites for small businesses, "A company slogan is a short phrase that follows your brand name in advertisements, business cards, and other marketing materials. It can be a powerful marketing tool when done right. A slogan's purpose is to reinforce your brand's identity."

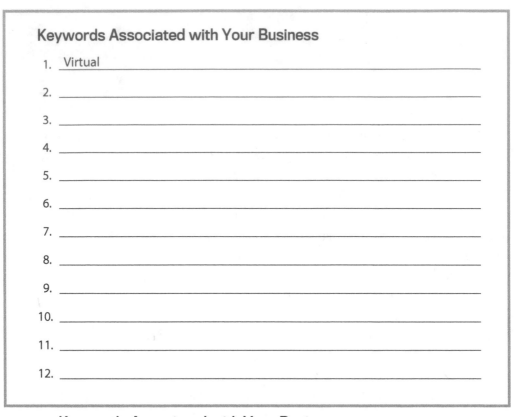

FIGURE 3–1: **Keywords Associated with Your Business**

Again, as you're brainstorming your company's slogan, be creative. Focus on coming up with a short phrase that's simple, memorable, differentiates your business, and elicits a positive thought or emotion.

The right slogan will help people instantly identify your business. When you see or hear slogans like "Just do it," "A diamond is forever," "Think different," "Finger lickin' good," or "The ultimate driving machine," what likely comes to mind are Nike, De Beers, Apple, KFC, and BMW, respectively—these are some of the most popular and successful slogans in history.

Your Company's Logo

While a name and slogan rely on words to convey information about your company, your logo is a visual representation of your company and its brand. As a startup, it's vital that your company logo look professional. It should also be memorable and appeal to your intended audience.

► Take Advantage of Free Company Naming Tools

Many marketing agencies specialize in creating company and brand names for their clients, but their services can be expensive. There are a number of websites, however, that will also assist you in brainstorming the perfect name for your business—for free. These sites ask you for words or phrases related to an industry, the work you do, or an emotion, for example, and then instantly generate potential business names.

A few of these business name generation services include:

- ► BNG (Business Name Generator): https://businessnamegenerator.com/
- ► Namelix: https://namelix.com
- ► Shopify Business Name Generator: https://www.shopify.com/tools/business-name-generator
- ► Squadhelp: https://www.squadhelp.com/business-name-generator
- ► WPBeginner: https://www.wpbeginner.com/tools/business-name-generator

A company logo can be a simple graphics-only design, or it can display your company name using a specific font, style, and color in a way that makes it visually unique.

It's a good idea to hire a professional graphic designer or illustrator to create your company's logo. The least expensive option is to hire a freelance graphic designer on a service like Upwork (https://www.upwork.com/), Fiverr (https://www.fiverr.com/), or Freelancer (https://www.freelancer.com/). Based on the designer's skill level and experience and the intricacy of your logo design, expect to pay anywhere from $50 to $300.

Once the logo is finalized and been delivered to you in a digital format that you can copy and use as needed, make sure you obtain a release in writing from the graphic designer that states you (or your business) own the artwork outright, and that they do not retain any legal rights or ownership to the copyright and/or trademark associated with the logo.

tip

When negotiating the price of having a logo created from scratch, make sure the graphic designer/illustrator agrees to create an initial set of five to ten rough designs for you to choose from, and then allows for a predetermined number of edits or alterations to the design you select. Pay a flat fee for the project, as opposed to an hourly rate.

Ten Logo Design Strategies

As you're working with a graphic designer to create your company logo, consider these ten strategies to help you design it:

1. Keep the design simple.
2. Choose the color or color scheme carefully. It should appeal to your target clients and not be too harsh or distracting. The colors should also be easy to match when creating other visual assets or types of online content.
3. It should convey an authoritative and professional tone.
4. Consider how the logo will look in color, in black and white, and when displayed in various sizes. You will be using it on your website, on letterhead, on business cards, in social media account profiles, in ads, and in countless other places.
5. Make sure the design is timeless, not following a current trend, or it will age poorly.
6. The logo should work seamlessly with the rest of your company's brand and brand elements.

▶ File the Appropriate Copyright or Trademark for Your Logo

Before you start using your logo, make sure it does not infringe on another company's copyright or trademark. Start by visiting the USPTO website (https://www.uspto.gov/trademarks/search). Another option is to hire a trademark attorney to handle the search (which could cost a few hundred dollars). If you infringe on another company's copyright or trademark with your logo, you'll likely be sued and wind up with hefty legal fees, so it might be worth the upfront costs.

Next, before you start using the logo publicly, it's good business strategy to apply for your own copyright and/or trademark based on its design. This is something you can do yourself. Go to the United States Patent and Trademark Office's website (https://www.uspto.gov/trademarks/basics) and U.S. Copyright Office site (https://www.copyright.gov), as needed. Another option involves using a company, such as LegalZoom (https://www.legalzoom.com). You'll need to pay for their services, as well as the required filing fees, but it streamlines the filing process and will help you avoid costly mistakes.

The most expensive option is to hire a trademark attorney. The best way to find one is through a referral, by contacting the state bar association, or by doing a search on LinkedIn, for example.

7. It should help to create or convey your company's vibe (i.e., how you want people to feel about your company).

8. Consider mixing a relevant image, icon, and/or shape with your company's name, displayed in a font and type style that make it unique.

9. Make sure the logo helps define your brand identity. Even if it does not include your company name, it will often be displayed in conjunction with your company name and slogan.

10. Consider the logo from the point of view of your prospective clients. Don't focus on just your personal taste.

Choose Your Domain Name

Your company's unique domain name (also known as a website address or URL) is how people will find your website on the internet. Your URL will begin with "http://" or "https://" and end with a website extension, such as ".com."

The difference between "http://" and "https://" is the type of encryption and security the website uses. The *s* in "https://" stands for *secure* and is mainly used for ecommerce websites or websites that collect information from visitors.

Website addresses most commonly end with a ".com" extension, although there are more than 300 different extensions available (such as .biz, .info, .org, .net, .io, .website, .accountant, .agency, .associates, and .design). While you may be able to do some clever marketing with a domain name that ends in a less common extension, most people automatically type ".com" at the end of a domain when manually entering a URL.

Thus, even if you heavily promote that your company's domain name is "www. YourCompanyName.biz," more often than not, people will type "www.YourCompanyName. com" into their web browser. In other words, if you choose a domain name ending in ".biz," you will also want to acquire that same name ending in ".com" and redirect any traffic that goes there to your website. Otherwise, the company or organization that owns it will likely end up receiving web traffic that was intended for your company.

As a small business owner, you want your domain name to include your company name (i.e., www.YourCompanyName.com). If someone already owns that domain name, seriously consider choosing a different company name.

As you brainstorm domain names for your website, use these strategies:

▶ Keep the domain name short—ideally 15 characters or less (not counting the "www." and ".com" or other extension).

▶ Make sure it's easy to spell and pronounce.

▶ It should be memorable.

▶ It must be unique and cannot violate anyone else's trademark or copyright.

▶ It should mesh with your brand.

▶ Avoid hyphens or underscores ("-" or "_").

▶ Consider the most likely typos when entering your domain name and register those names as well.

The next step is to determine if your chosen domain name is available. The easiest way to do this is to visit any domain name registrar and enter it in the search field. Five of the more popular domain name registrars are:

1. Domain.com: https://www.domain.com/
2. GoDaddy: https://www.godaddy.com/
3. Google Domains: https://domains.google/
4. Name.com: https://www.name.com/
5. Network Solutions: https://www.networksolutions.com/

For each domain name you register, you'll pay an annual fee. Depending on the registrar and on how many years you pay for in advance, the annual fee will be anywhere from $8 to $20 per name. Keep in mind, you can register as many domain names as you wish and have all of them direct traffic to the same website or to a specific page on your website.

Focus on Website Design

Once you've registered your domain name(s), the next step is to choose a website hosting service, and then create and publish your website. Website hosting fees vary greatly. Avoid using a free hosting service, as these are automatically populated with ads, detracting from your professional image.

And it's essential that your website look professional. From a visual standpoint, the design should be based around your brand and nicely cater to its intended audience. Using website design tools, you can create a professional-looking website by yourself, with no graphic design or programming experience. If you go with this option, you'll want to use a website design tool that offers design templates. These are web page designs created by professional graphic designers and website designers, but

tip ⓘ

Many companies, like GoDaddy or Bluehost, offer domain name registration, website hosting services, and website design/do-it-yourself website creation tools all together. You can pay for these services on an a la carte basis or save money by bundling them together.

that you can fully customize to suit your website. Some website design tools don't rely on templates but instead allow you to drag-and-drop pre-made elements into your website.

Finding the Right Hosting Service for Your Website

When choosing a hosting service, look for one that offers:

- ▶ An unlimited number of web pages
- ▶ Automatic backup
- ▶ Plenty of (or unlimited/unmetered) storage space
- ▶ No bandwidth limitations (especially if you'll be publishing video or audio content)
- ▶ Integration with popular website development/design tools (such as WordPress)
- ▶ Integration with popular software applications, such as QuickBooks (if you're operating an ecommerce website that sells products or your services) or a scheduling application (such as Calendly) if a prospective client wants to book time with you
- ▶ An SSL certificate option (giving you a secure "https://" URL)
- ▶ Ecommerce tools (if you choose to sell items or services directly from your site)

A hosting service should also offer real-time analytics (so you can track site traffic) as well as 24/7 customer service (via phone, online chat, or email). Seek out a hosting service that's well-established and reliable. Uptime rates (meaning the time the service is available to its users) of 98 to 99.98 percent are considered standard. Site visitors will also typically experience faster load times when your web host has many servers in your home country.

Design Your Site

Once you've secured a domain name and lined up a company to host your website, the next step is to design your site. Ideally, you should work with a website designer or graphic designer to ensure the result looks highly professional and works well regardless of which browser, PC, laptop, or mobile device the visitor is using to access your site. However, most of these services offer tools that allow you to design your own website using a template (with no programming required).

When it comes to designing your website, you'll need to decide what content you want to include and how to organize it. As soon as someone types your domain name into their browser (or clicks on a link to your website), they'll be taken to your homepage. From here, they can view your main menu, which gives them access to the other major areas of your site.

Take a look at the websites of at least a dozen different virtual assistants and VA agencies. Not only will this give you a good idea of the type of content to include, but it will also help you determine the types of features and functions you may want to incorporate into your own site.

In addition to the homepage, which should include content designed to entice the visitor and provide them with a quick summary about who you are and what you do, individual web pages and functions you should consider adding to your website include:

▶ *About Us.* This page should include a detailed description of your company that discusses why it was founded, its philosophy, and an overview of its specialties. It should also feature short bios of the company's leaders. If you're running a one-person operation, post a bio about yourself that discusses your education, work history, key accomplishments, and skill set. You can also include your mission statement and anything else you think potential clients will find relevant.

▶ *Benefits.* For companies or individuals who have never hired or worked with a virtual assistant before, this page can showcase how a client can benefit from working with your company. Focus on how you can save your client time and money and how you prioritize client confidentiality and privacy, for example.

▶ *Client Testimonials.* Once you're established and have a few clients, ask them for some short testimonials and post them on this page.

▶ *Contact Us/Schedule a Call.* Your email address, phone number, and mailing address should be prominently displayed on every page on your site. The Contact Us page, however, should display this information plus a form that visitors can fill out to receive a prompt response. A typical form will ask for their name, email address, phone number, and a brief message explaining what they're interested in talking about.

▶ *Live Chat.* Some websites offer a live chat feature that allows visitors to communicate in real-time via instant messaging with you or a representative from your company. Live chat is typically only available during business hours.

▶ *Pricing.* Display your hourly rates or package rates if they're fixed. Some virtual assistants choose to offer a "Get a Quote" button instead, so they can adjust their pricing to meet a potential client's needs.

▶ *Resources.* If you have free articles, videos, or content that you want to share with prospective and existing clients, this can be offered here.

▶ *Services.* Use this page to display a comprehensive menu of services that you offer. You may opt to

tip ⓘ

When creating text-based content for your website, such as on the Services page, make sure it can be easily printed by sizing it to fit a standard letter-size page (especially when a web browser's Reader or Reader View mode is used), or by making it downloadable as a nicely formatted PDF.

display service headings, like "Social Media and Digital Marketing," "Administrative Assistance," "Executive Assistance," "Bookkeeping," and/or "Website Design," and then display a bulleted list of specific services offered in each category.

Creating Content for Your Site

As you're writing text and choosing content for each page on your site, keep these ten strategies in mind:

1. The content should be concise and focus only on information your visitors will want to know. Answer questions like who, what, where, when, why, and how much? Focus on addressing the wants and needs of your visitors, answering their questions before they're asked, and explaining how you can help eliminate challenges or solve problems the potential client is facing.

2. Proofread your work. Your website should contain zero spelling, punctuation, grammatical, or factual errors. If a potential client notices a mistake on your site, it will immediately tarnish your professional credibility and could prevent them from hiring you.

3. Sell yourself and your services using upbeat and professional language.

4. Most online visitors have a very short attention span. If your website (and each page of your site) does not capture their interest within five to ten seconds, they'll likely go elsewhere. Likewise, if a web page is too wordy or too cluttered, they'll get bored and click away.

5. Avoid pop-ups and distracting graphics and animations. Eliminate anything that takes their attention away from your core message.

6. Keep your font(s), type styles, and color scheme consistent with your brand.

7. Make sure each web page is formatted and programmed to support all popular web browsers

tip

When it comes to website design, you don't need to reinvent the wheel. Look online for website templates already created for your type of business, and then focus on customizing the template rather than trying to create a website from scratch. For example, search Google or Bing for "virtual assistant business web page template."

The Colorlib website (https://colorlib.com/) has an article offering ten website templates for virtual assistant businesses. Also check the WordPress theme/template directory for more options (https://wordpress.org/).

and reformats itself automatically based on the screen size of the computer or mobile device being used. For example, all text and graphics should be easy to view on a smartphone screen.

8. Use plenty of white space in your design and avoid clutter. Some of the most successful websites in existence have a plain white background with no visual distractions. Keep your design simple and professional. Examples of websites that expertly utilize white space include Google.com, Apple.com, and Amazon.com.

9. Make sure the website is easy and intuitive to navigate. Anticipate what information your potential clients will want, and make it easy to find from your homepage.

10. Incorporate a call to action on each web page, such as "Click here for more information," "Click here to schedule a call," or "Click here to get a quote."

Remember, when creating content for your website, you can use text, photos, graphics, animations, audio, and video. When deciding which type of content to use, choose the one that will communicate your message to your visitors best, and most quickly. If you can condense the information in three full screens' worth of text down into a 30-second video clip, that will be easier for your clients—and they will be much more likely to watch a short video than read a long document, however well it is written.

To enhance the visual appeal of your website, include relevant photos or graphics. For a very low fee per image, you can download and use professional photography from stock photo agencies. Some of these agencies include:

▶ Getty Images (https://www.gettyimages.com/)
▶ iStock (https://www.istockphoto.com/)
▶ Shutterstock (https://www.shutterstock.com/)

You are not allowed to use someone else's photography, graphics, or artwork without written permission from the copyright owner.

Use Branded Social Media Content

Chapter 6 focuses on the various ways you can use social media to promote your business and find new clients. As you'll discover, becoming active on relevant social media platforms and establishing a social media presence for your company is essential.

> **tip**
>
> Website design may not be your area of expertise, but there are many VAs who do offer this type of service and have many years of experience as website designers. By hiring your own virtual assistant to help create and manage your website, not only will you get the job done right, but the person helping you will understand your business, and you will be building a relationship with another VA who might be able to refer clients to you in the future.

At the very least, you'll want to create a Facebook page for your business that's separate from your personal Facebook page—along with personal and business accounts on Twitter and LinkedIn.

As you create content to share with your followers, subscribers, and "friends" on social media, the messaging and visuals should be consistent with your company's brand. For example, use your company logo as a profile photo on your company Facebook page, LinkedIn page, and Twitter feed. In the description field of the account profile, enter your company's slogan.

You can use social media as a sales, promotions, and marketing tool for your business, but avoid the hard sell. Instead, provide free content, advice, or answers to questions that showcase your expertise, and be sure to include your company's website address. From a visual and content standpoint, make sure whatever you post is appropriate and interesting to potential (and existing) clients, and that it's compatible with your brand.

Use Personalized Email Accounts

Obtaining a free email account (from Google, Yahoo!, or Microsoft, for example) is easy. However, for someone operating a business, it's not a good idea. As soon as anyone who is the least bit tech-savvy sees an email address ending in @gmail.com, @yahoo.com, or @ outlook.com, they know it's a free account.

Depending on which domain name registrar or hosting service you use, you can pay an extra monthly or annual fee for one or more email addresses that include your name

► **Take Advantage of the Social Media Services Your Prospective Clients Already Use**

The various social media platforms all have free information and tutorials online to help you learn how to create business pages, effectively promote your business, or advertise on their services. Below are some links that will help you learn more:

- ► Facebook: https://www.facebook.com/business
- ► Twitter: https://business.twitter.com/en/basics/intro-twitter-for-business.html
- ► LinkedIn: https://business.linkedin.com/marketing-solutions/linkedin-pages
- ► Instagram: https://business.instagram.com/getting-started
- ► Pinterest: https://business.pinterest.com
- ► TikTok: https://www.tiktok.com/business/en-US

and domain name: YourName@YourDomainName.com. In terms of developing a professional image and maintaining the appearance of a legitimate business that you want people to take seriously, personalized email addresses are definitely a good investment. Some website hosting services include one or more personalized email addresses.

An alternative to going through your domain name registrar or website hosting service for your business email address(es) are online companies such as IONOS (www.ionos.com) or GoDaddy (www.godaddy.com) that offer professional email as a stand-alone service for between $1 and $9 per month, per email account.

Make sure you choose an email hosting service that offers plenty of storage space for each user. At least 5GB of space should be adequate (at least initially). You also want to be able to send ad-free emails, and access and manage your email accounts through webmail or a popular email client app on your computer and mobile devices. Each email account should automatically sync between all your devices, and they should offer a customizable/adjustable spam filter and virus protection.

As you'll discover in Chapter 4, as a virtual assistant it's pretty much mandatory that you have your own Microsoft 365 or Microsoft Office account, so you can use Word, Excel, PowerPoint, Outlook, and other applications that are so common in the business world.

tip

After setting up one email address using the format YourName@ YourDomainName.com, you can often set up alias email addresses. These are alternate email addresses that still go to your inbox. For example, one alias might be Info@ YourDomainName.com or CustomerService@ YourDomainName.com. However, if you want multiple people to have their own email addresses with the format UserName@ YourDomainName.com, you will have to set up (and often pay for) separate email accounts. The process and cost will depend on your email service provider.

Microsoft, along with many third-party email service providers, offers bundles that include a Microsoft 365 subscription and a personalized email address for a flat monthly or annual fee (starting as low as $4.50 per month).

Obtaining personalized email addresses for your business allows you to easily separate your personal and business emails and gives you a more professional image. If you're serious about establishing a credible brand for your business, this is one investment you should make right at the start.

Don't Forget Letterhead and Business Cards

As the job title suggests, most (if not all) of your work will be done from the comfort of your home office, or wherever you set up your computer or mobile device.

But even though most of your work takes place online, that doesn't mean you won't have uses for old-fashioned promotional material: printed letterhead, business cards, envelopes, promotional/sales brochures, postcards, paper invoices, contracts, personalized greeting cards, and other documents you'll be sharing with your clients (or prospective clients) via hard copy. All these should prominently showcase your company name, slogan, and logo, along with your contact information, using the same fonts, type styles, and color schemes as your website.

Again, work with a graphic designer to help create your letterhead, business cards, printed brochures, and related documents. You will use them often, especially when you're mailing out information to prospective clients or participating in in-person networking events and/or trade shows. And don't forget about the quality of the paper and cardstock you use to print them. Features like multicolor raised printing will add to your credibility by enhancing their professional appearance.

In addition to local print shops and office supply stores with an in-house print shop (such as Staples or OfficeMax), many printing services offer a wide range of products you can order online, such as VistaPrint (https://www.vistaprint.com/), PsPrint by Deluxe (https://www.psprint.com/), and MOO (https://www.moo.com/). Some offer free or low-cost design services as well.

You can further expand your brand by incorporating your logo, slogan, and other promotional elements into your custom-formatted emails, invoices, proposals, estimates, and other documentation you'll be creating and sharing online. For example, you can design and set up branded email signatures to appear at the bottom of your emails.

An email signature can be customized to include your name, job title, company name, slogan, email address, phone number(s), mailing address, website address, and social media usernames, for example.

Most email client software applications allow you to create one or more email signatures. If you want to add a more professional design element to your email signature, you can pay a service like WiseStamp (https://webapp.wisestamp.com/editor) or Exclaimer (https://www.exclaimer.com/lp/en/email-signatures/), which makes this process very easy.

fun fact

Incorporating an email signature into your outgoing emails is yet another way you can convey a highly professional image and extend your brand.

Your Business Phone Number

As someone operating your own virtual assistant business, it is essential that your business have its own phone number that is separate from your home phone number and/or personal mobile phone number.

There are multiple ways to establish a separate phone number for your business. The easiest (and often least expensive) is to obtain a virtual phone number via a Voice over Internet Protocol (VoIP) service provider. VoIP lets you make phone calls using an internet connection rather than a phone line, so you can get a new phone number through an online company, often very cheaply.

Popular VoIP service providers that cater to small businesses include:

▶ 8x8: https://www.8x8.com/

▶ Dialpad: https://www.dialpad.com/

▶ Freshdesk: https://www.freshworks.com/freshcaller-cloud-pbx/

▶ Google Voice: https://cloud.google.com/voice

▶ Grasshopper: https://grasshopper.com/

▶ RingCentral: https://www.ringcentral.com/

▶ Skype: https://www.skype.com/en/

▶ Vonage: https://www.vonage.com/

These services will provide your business with a unique phone number that can be forwarded automatically to your existing phone. You can also answer and make calls using a special app on your smartphone, tablet, or computer.

As you're setting up the phone number for your business, make sure it includes services and features you'll need, like customizable caller ID for outgoing calls (so your company's name and/or phone number appears on the caller ID display of the person you're calling), as well as call forwarding, call waiting, incoming caller ID, conference calling, and voice mail (with the ability to custom-record your outgoing message). These are all part of expanding your brand while interacting with your clients.

When choosing a phone service, keep in mind that calling features and functions can vary greatly. Figure out what you need, and then shop around for a service that offers those features at an affordable monthly rate. Things like unlimited domestic calls should be a standard feature in any calling package.

Another business option is a toll-free 800 or 888 number for your clients, which allows them to call you for free. While in the past businesses used toll-free numbers to help customers or clients avoid long-distance charges, these days they're more of an optional branding tool to help convey the image of a well-established and legitimate business.

▶ Consider Hiring a Virtual Receptionist for Your Business

In terms of building a positive image with (prospective) clients, instead of relying on an automated voice mail service when you're unable to answer your phone, consider using a virtual receptionist (a person or agency that specializes in answering incoming phone calls on behalf of their clients, routing calls to the appropriate people, or taking messages for the intended recipient).

Yes, this costs more than voice mail, but if you cater to higher-end clients, the investment could be worth it, because most people prefer to leave a message with a human being rather than a machine. Your brand's value would increase by providing your clients with this enhanced customer service experience.

Intelligent Office is a franchisor of its virtual reception and flexible work space business. According to their website, "A virtual receptionist performs tasks like answering incoming calls, scheduling, faxing, invoicing, and other admin responsibilities—all from their remote or home office."

Working with an independent virtual receptionist to answer and direct your incoming calls might provide you with a professional networking experience and potential referrals for your business as you develop the relationship. Several of the many virtual receptionist agencies you could hire include:

- ▶ AnswerForce: https://www.answerforce.com/
- ▶ Intelligent Office: https://www.intelligentoffice.com/phone-answering-service
- ▶ My Receptionist: https://myreceptionist.com/
- ▶ Ruby: https://www.ruby.com/

Another perk for small businesses that offer a toll-free number is that you can automatically capture the incoming caller's phone number (and often their name), even if they have caller ID blocked when making an outgoing call.

It's Time to Set Up Your Work Space

As a virtual assistant, you can work from anywhere, if you can complete the tasks assigned to you by your clients. Often, however, you'll likely be working from home. The next chapter focuses on gathering the equipment, online tools, and software you'll need to establish your home office and operate your business. You'll also discover strategies you can use when working from home to set up your work space (even if you're on a tight budget) that'll help make you more productive.

The Equipment You'll Need

Regardless of which niche you decide to focus on as a virtual assistant, the equipment you'll need to operate your homebased business is rather straightforward, and the cost is relatively low in terms of initial investment. Of course, as your business becomes successful, you always have the option to upgrade.

Depending on which services you'll be offering to your clients, the specialized equipment you'll need, including software, will vary greatly. For example, you'll likely need to acquire and use the online collaboration and virtual communication tools that your clients are already using. As a result, you'll likely need to become proficient at and have access to a wide range of apps to stay compatible with your clients. Zoom, Microsoft Teams, Skype, and Google Meet, for example, all offer video calling and virtual meeting spaces. As you onboard each new client, you'll need to adapt to their virtual communication preferences.

In addition to providing an overview of the equipment you'll likely need to set up and operate your homebased virtual assistant business, this chapter focuses on how to create the ideal home office environment for yourself—one that will provide comfort, allow you to stay organized, and potentially help you maximize your time and productivity.

Establish Your Home Office and Set Up Your Work Space

When running a business from your home, you'll need to allocate a separate space to accommodate it. As you're just getting started, your dining room table or a small desk in the corner of your bedroom might do, but soon you'll likely find this work space is small, uncomfortable, and easy to outgrow. For example, if your dining room table is your primary desk, you'll need to pack up your entire office every evening at dinnertime, and then set everything back up again the next morning.

Ideally, you want to establish your home office in a separate room (such as a spare room, guest bedroom, finished basement, finished attic, or climate-controlled garage), so you can create your own quiet and comfortable work space with a door you can close. Depending on where you live, you might not have a lot of options in terms of available space, but even a decent walk-in closet might be better than the dining room table.

Selecting Your Work Space

Transforming a portion of your home into a comfortable and productive work space can be a challenge. When choosing where to locate your office, consider the following:

fun fact ☺

According to OSHA, most people are most comfortable and productive when the temperature is between 70 and 73 degrees Fahrenheit, with the humidity somewhere between 20 and 60 percent. OSHA recommends employers maintain workplace temperatures between 68 and 76 degrees Fahrenheit.

► *Climate control.* Being able to maintain a constant, comfortable temperature, as well as good air quality, is important. If the air is too dry, too humid, contains mold, or has harsh smells, this can all negatively impact your health and productivity. To improve air quality, you might want to use a humidifier, dehumidifier, or air purifier in your work space. If you're working from a basement, attic, or garage, consider installing a smoke and carbon monoxide detector as well.

► *Décor.* From an aesthetic standpoint, you want your work space to be visually calming and decorated to your liking. Placing live plants in your home office, for example, will improve almost any décor and can enhance the air quality. Displaying your favorite artwork or photographs also adds a personalized touch to your work space that can help improve your mood.

► *Electricity.* Make sure your home office has access to multiple electrical outlets. Running a lot of extension cords through your home or connecting too many power strips (and/or power adapters) to a single outlet isn't safe.

► *Internet connectivity.* For your main work computer, a direct connection to your modem or wireless router will likely provide a better connection than wifi. However, if you are relying on wifi, make sure the signal is strong in your work area and the bandwidth can accommodate your needs as well as your family's—especially when you're making a video call, your children are playing online games, and your spouse is streaming a movie via Netflix.

> **warning** ⚠
>
> To avoid eyestrain and headaches, adjustable "natural white" lighting will serve you well. Use LED or incandescent lightbulbs, and keep in mind that the position of your lighting is as important as the brightness.
>
> If a light is shining into your eyes while you're staring at a computer monitor, it will cause eyestrain, for example. Ideally, you want your home office to be well lit with even lighting, with no harsh shadows or bright lights directly in your eyes.

► *Lighting.* A room with a window will provide natural light during the day, which is good for your mental health. Being able to open the window provides fresh air. If you're relying on artificial lighting, avoid lights that are too bright, too dim, or that flicker (such as fluorescent lighting).

► *Noise control.* Especially if you have kids and/or pets, you need a quiet space that you can close off from the rest of your house during virtual meetings and phone calls, or just when you need to concentrate.

▶ *Storage space.* Whether for paper documents and files, office supplies, or other tools and equipment, it's important to keep everything you'll need during your workday close by and convenient. Especially if you're working from a small space, the creative use of storage will allow you to keep your work space clean and clutter free.

▶ *Room to work.* In addition to at least one full-size office desk (with plenty of surface area and drawers for storage), you'll want room for a full-size office chair, lamp(s), storage/filing cabinets, a trash can, and space for your equipment (a computer, printer, desk phone, etc.).

▶ *Your work process (work flow).* Everyone's work habits are different. If you have spent time working in a traditional office and know what makes you productive in that environment, for instance, you'll likely want to duplicate that work process in your home office.

Choose the Right Office Furniture

The two most important pieces of furniture in your home office are your desk and desk chair. Measure your office space carefully and make sure you have ample room for a full-size desk (with a large desktop). Unless you opt to go with a more costly adjustable stand-up/sit-down desk, make sure it's a standard height, so it offers comfort, plenty of room to work, and efficiency.

> **tip** ⓘ
>
> If you only have the budget to invest in one really good piece of office furniture, spend it on your office chair.

Also consider where you'll be placing your computer's monitor. Make sure the monitor will be at the appropriate height and distance from your face.

Because you'll likely be spending eight to ten hours per day (or more) working from your home office, choosing the perfect office chair is an important decision. Do not use a standard metal folding chair or a dining room chair. Instead, invest in a desk chair that provides comfort and support for your neck, shoulders, back, legs, arms, and wrists.

Your desk chair should offer:

▶ Adjustable back and lumbar support

▶ Ergonomic design

▶ Adjustable height

▶ The ability to swivel and recline

▶ Adjustable armrests that provide ample support when using a keyboard or mouse

tip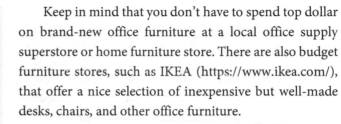

Don't feel like you have to undergo massive home renovations to accommodate your new work-from-home situation. Just focus on being productive from the work space that's available to you.

Keep in mind that you don't have to spend top dollar on brand-new office furniture at a local office supply superstore or home furniture store. There are also budget furniture stores, such as IKEA (https://www.ikea.com/), that offer a nice selection of inexpensive but well-made desks, chairs, and other office furniture.

You can also save a lot of money by purchasing used office furniture. Try searching for "used office furniture" and see what's available locally on eBay or Craigslist, and check the listings on Facebook Marketplace. You might also be able to borrow furniture from family, friends, or neighbors.

In terms of office chairs, perhaps the most popular chair in the corporate world is the Herman Miller Aeron chair. It sells on the company website for $1,395 (not including optional accessories). However, you can often find the same chair, in excellent used condition, for less than $300.

Gather the Equipment You'll Need

Once you have the furniture in your home office set up, you'll need to populate your work space with the equipment you need to do your work. For most virtual assistants, this includes:

- ▶ Desktop and/or laptop computer
- ▶ Printer, scanner, copier, and fax machine (or an all-in-one desktop unit). A scanner with a flatbed and document feeder is ideal for creating digital documents and files to avoid paper clutter.
- ▶ Laser printer or full-color specialty printer
- ▶ High-end webcam (ideally 4K HD quality)
- ▶ Landline phone (optional)
- ▶ External hard drive(s)
- ▶ Internet equipment (modem, wireless router, and wifi signal booster, if needed)

warning

When setting up your home office, avoid adding extras like a coffee machine, small refrigerator, or TV set. You'll want to take short breaks throughout your day, and walking to your kitchen for a cup of coffee or a snack gives your body a chance to stretch and gives you a few minutes to clear your mind. A TV in your home office will just be a distraction, especially if you wind up getting hooked on soap operas or leave a 24-hour cable news channel playing all day.

▶ Mobile devices (smartphone and/or tablet)

▶ Wireless headset to enhance sound quality during phone calls, video calls, and virtual meetings

You do not need to go out and invest in a brand-new, top-of-the-line Windows PC or Mac unless you'll be doing very specialized work that requires the latest and greatest microprocessors and graphics card. A computer that's one or two years old (bought used) can handle tasks like word processing, database/spreadsheet management, and making video/voice calls using VoIP.

Similarly, if you don't have room for a flatbed scanner, there are apps that will allow you to use your mobile device's rear-facing camera as a scanner, so you can create PDF files from any documents using your smartphone. To find a scanner app, visit the App Store (for iPhones) or the Google Play Store (for Androids) and search for "scanner."

The Software Tools You'll Likely Need

Again, regardless of your chosen niche as a VA, some of the essential software tools you'll need include:

▶ A Microsoft 365 (or Microsoft Office) subscription, which gives you unlimited access to Microsoft applications, such as Word, Excel, PowerPoint, Skype, and Outlook from all your computers and mobile devices.

▶ Google Workspace, which is another popular suite of office applications that includes Gmail, Calendar, Meet, Chat, Drive, Docs, Sheets, Slides, Forms, and more.

▶ A bookkeeping/accounting application. While you have multiple options, the one used by many small businesses (and which is supported by virtually all accountants) is Intuit's QuickBooks (http://quickbooks.intuit.com).

> **warning** ⚠
>
> While free office suite software, such as iWork from Apple, is available for all Macs, iPhones, and iPads, and these applications create files that are compatible with Microsoft Office and Google Workspace, you're better off relying on the actual applications used by your clients. Both Microsoft and Google offer extremely affordable subscription rates for their office suites.
>
> If you're working on a tight budget, one free alternative to Microsoft Office is the Apache OpenOffice software, which is available as open-source software for Windows PCs and Macs. You can download and install OpenOffice by visiting www.openoffice.org/.

▶ A customizable time-tracking application. Because you'll most likely be billing your clients based on the time you spend working for them, it's important to track and keep detailed records of every minute of your day you spend catering to each client.

▶ The video calling and virtual meeting application(s) used by your clients.

▶ The messaging applications (such as Slack) used by your clients.

▶ A customizable time management/scheduling/calendar application. Which one you choose should be based on your workstyle, needs, and personal preference.

tip

A few examples of popular and highly customizable project management applications include Monday.com (https://monday.com/), Zoho Projects (https://www.zoho.com/), FreshBooks (www.freshbooks.com/), and Smartsheet (www.smartsheet.com/).

▶ A CRM application to help you manage all details and information pertaining to your clients (and prospective clients). Again, which one you choose should be based on your workstyle, needs, and personal preference, as well as how many co-workers/employees need access to the database.

▶ PDF file creation, editing, annotating, storage, and management software, such as Adobe Acrobat or Adobe Acrobat PDF Pack (https://www.adobe.com/) or PDF Expert (https://pdfexpert.com/).

▶ Project management software. Choose a customizable application that adapts best to your personal work flow and your need to juggle and manage multiple projects for various clients simultaneously.

▶ A secure cloud-based file sharing service for data backup, file sharing, and online collaboration. You have many options for this, such as Dropbox, Apple iCloud, Microsoft OneDrive, Google Drive, or Box.

tip

The Hubstaff Blog published a comprehensive article in December 2020, "The 41 Best Virtual Assistant Software Tools in 2021," which you'll likely find useful. Read it here: https://blog.hubstaff.com/.

Take Advantage of Apps Designed Specifically for Virtual Assistants

In addition to stand-alone applications designed to handle specific tasks (like Clockify for time tracking), there are all-in-one applications designed specifically for the operation and management of virtual assistant businesses. You will only need one such application (running on all your computers and accessible from your mobile devices), but there are several to choose from, including Adminja (www.getadminja.com/) and HoneyBook (www.honeybook.com/virtual-assistant-software).

The following is an exclusive interview with Bryan Lewis, founder and designer of the popular Adminja software, which is currently being used by thousands of virtual assistants throughout the world. In this interview, he offers valuable tips and strategies on how VAs can best use the software, along with advice about how someone can become a top-notch virtual assistant.

What inspired you to create the Adminja application specifically for virtual assistants?

Bryan Lewis: I used to run a website design and development shop in Chicago. At the time, I had a virtual assistant that I hired through one of the largest agencies in the state. Having a VA transformed my business in terms of helping me with the little things and staying on track with my schedule. One day, after two and a half years, the agency contacted me out of the blue and said they were shutting down their business.

I was in a state of panic and immediately contacted my VA directly, who was also in a state of panic because she no longer had a job. I wound up hiring her directly. While she was working with the agency, they handled billing, client acquisition, sales, and management. All she needed to do was the clients' work. I wound up helping her establish her own virtual assistant business, and I also helped her former co-workers set up their virtual assistant businesses.

In the process of assisting multiple VAs to establish their independent businesses, I learned that at the time, nobody was building or offering tools specifically for virtual assistants. They were being forced to use many different tools and applications to manage their businesses and get their work done. Many of those tools were not compatible and didn't share or sync data with each other. I started learning what features and functions VAs wanted and needed in a single application, and that's how the concept for Adminja came about.

Adminja started out as an application designed to help VAs organize various types of information pertaining to their clients. Over time, it evolved into a single application that handles task management, project management, time tracking, billing, and client relationship management-related tasks.

How do you describe today's iteration of Adminja?

Lewis: It's an all-in-one, easy-to-use tool for managing your clients and staying on top of things. This application will help a VA keep their business on track and well-organized.

Unlike other project management tools, Adminja offers functionality for managing multiple clients, and all their projects, at once. For example, Adminja continuously generates time reports for clients automatically and keeps track of how much of a VA's time a client has remaining in their current plan or contract.

Is Adminja designed to be used by all virtual assistants, regardless of their niche or how many clients they're working with at any given time?

Lewis: Generally, Adminja works regardless of a VA's niche. This application is designed to handle the admin work associated with running a virtual assistant business. It does not handle the actual work or tasks a VA is hired to do for their clients. Adminja is for keeping track of your clients and the work you need to do and the work that you've done. It's great for managing and tracking your time, and then generating your invoices accordingly.

We've really put a lot of work into developing a customizable time-tracking tool that works nicely for any VA, regardless of the type of work they're doing. What Adminja is not designed to handle is bookkeeping or accounting, but it does share data with popular accounting/bookkeeping packages, like QuickBooks.

When someone creates an invoice using Adminja, that information automatically gets transferred into QuickBooks, for example. Adminja integrates with a free tool called Zapier [https://zapier.com], which then integrates seamlessly with more than 2,000 other commonly used applications.

The Adminja application allows users to create Task Boards, Client Detail Boards, and Project Boards. How are these used and what sets them apart?

Lewis: A Client Detail Board is an advanced CRM application that allows you to collect and manage all sorts of information related to each of your clients. Basically, everything you need to know about a client, from their phone number to their birthday and even their shoe size, is kept in one place.

The Task Boards offer a flexible way for managing the different lists and tasks that you're responsible for handling for each client. This tool uses a similar, virtual card-like interface, like Trello, for example. The Project Boards allow a user to organize, track, and manage multiple projects for their various clients in a single place. We've built Adminja so each module is very customizable, based on the VA's existing work flow and work habits.

What's your biggest tip for someone first starting to use Adminja?

Lewis: The biggest tip I offer to new users of the software is to become very familiar with the different ways the built-in time tracker can be used. Capturing and tracking every minute of your time is essential to every virtual assistant, and this is something that many

VAs, especially those first starting out, do not do well. When you're not tracking your time properly, you're leaving money on the table and not getting paid for the work you're actually doing.

Typically, when someone begins using new software, it's necessary for them to adjust their work habits to accommodate that tool. Is this the case with Adminja?

Lewis: Once you understand how the time tracker and other functions of Adminja work, you'll quickly get into the habit of using the application as you go about your day-to-day work. I also recommend to new users that they install the optional Chrome web browser extension. Then, when doing something on the web using Chrome, it's very easy to access Adminja tools without having to first launch the application.

As a cloud-based tool, Adminja works on Windows PCs and Macs. Does it also work well with tablets and smartphones?

Lewis: The application will currently adapt to any size screen, whether you're using a desktop computer, laptop computer, or tablet. In late summer 2021, we introduced smartphone compatibility as well, so it works nicely with iPhones and Android-based mobile devices. This is handled via a web app that's used with a smartphone's web browser, as opposed to an installable mobile application.

What does an Adminja user need to know about the application's built-in security and privacy tools?

Lewis: This application was built using the Google Cloud platform, and we fully utilize Google's authentication systems. All data is encrypted in transit and at rest.

How long should it take someone who does not consider themselves too tech-savvy to get started using Adminja?

Lewis: After about 30 minutes, a new user will fully understand what the application is capable of and how it can be used to manage their virtual assistant business.

tip

To learn more about the security and privacy features and functions associated with Google Cloud, visit https://cloud.google.com/.

Like anything else, practice using the software will make someone proficient with its various tools, features, and functions. Our application is very easy to use. In terms of when a VA should start using the Adminja application, I recommend they begin using it at the same time they onboard their very first client.

We offer a free 30-day trial for Adminja. I suggest signing up for the free trial at the same time you launch your business. This allows you to get acquainted with the software when you don't yet have to deal with a client's needs. Then, if the trial period expires before you've landed your first client, wait until that point to begin your paid Adminja subscription.

Building long-term relationships with clients is a major key to a virtual assistant's success. How can the Adminja software help a VA build and manage these relationships?

Lewis: The biggest way Adminja helps with that is the automatic status reports feature. With our application, you can choose when and if a client will receive a customized status report, and what information will be included in that report. The reports are nicely formatted and can automatically be emailed to clients, which greatly improves communication between clients and VAs.

For example, the status report can include progress details pertaining to each separate project or task the VA is handling for that client, along with a time accounting, so if the client is on retainer or has pre-purchased a time-related package, they know exactly how much time has already been used and what was accomplished during that time. These reports can also help a client stay engaged with the VA, so they make better use of the VA's time that's available to them each week or month.

Aside from Adminja, what other applications do you recommend for a virtual assistant to operate and manage their business?

Lewis: An accounting package, such as QuickBooks [https://quickbooks.intuit.com/], Xero Accounting [https://www.xero.com/us/], or FreshBooks [https://www.freshbooks.com/], is important for keeping track of tax-related information and being able to create quarterly and annual reports for your accountant and the IRS.

If you're a graphic artist, you'll be using graphic design tools as well as Adminja. If you specialize in word processing, you may need to use Microsoft Word in addition to Adminja. Again, our software is designed to help you manage your virtual assistant business, not provide the tools for performing work for your clients.

tip

For a solo user, the subscription rate for Adminja (as of summer 2021) is $29.99 per month. For a team with at least five members, the rate is $10 per user per month. The Team version (marketed to VA agencies) includes a Team Manager module for managing multiple VAs. Visit the company's website (www.getadminja.com/) for more information about the application and to set up a free 30-day trial or a paid subscription.

What are some of the biggest mistakes you see virtual assistants making as they get started in this line of work?

Lewis: Giving away their time for free. I see this way too often, even after they've been working for a client for several months. It's great to be generous with your time every now and then, but it is not something you should get into the habit of doing all the time. Your clients will begin to take advantage of your generosity. If you're providing value to a client, that client should be paying for your work.

I also see communication mistakes happen often. Don't be afraid to have those more difficult conversations with your clients. When a client comes to you with a new project, for example, and asks what it's going to cost, don't hold back in providing a truthful and accurate answer. Always be upfront with your clients.

How do you see the role of a virtual assistant changing over the next three to five years?

Lewis: The Covid-19 pandemic has helped the virtual assistant industry grow, but the business model has stayed pretty much the same. I don't see it changing too much anytime soon. There are just more clients than ever before looking to work with VAs.

I've seen niching become more popular with VAs recently, and I see this becoming an ongoing trend. I currently see a fine line between the work of a virtual assistant that's hired by a company on a long-term basis vs. a freelancer who is hired to handle just one specific task or project for a client. The Adminja application works best for VAs looking to develop and manage long-term relationships with their clients.

As the business model for VAs does evolve over time, we'll adapt the Adminja application accordingly. For example, in summer 2021, we redesigned the client billing module from scratch and incorporated direct invoicing and Stripe payment integration [https://stripe.com], so VAs can get paid electronically through the Stripe billing system.

The Next Steps in Launching Your Own Virtual Assistant Business

One of the biggest challenges virtual assistants face is setting their rates. If you undercharge for your work, you run the risk of losing credibility and the respect of your clients, but if you charge too much, potential clients will seek out VAs willing to work for a more competitive rate.

The next chapter offers some practical advice on how to set your rates so that they're fair, competitive, and in line with what other VAs are charging—depending on your skill set, experience, the type of work you'll be performing, and the types of clients you plan to work with. You'll learn more about the different fee structures that virtual assistants typically use, and based on the experiences of well-established virtual assistants, discover what works best and why.

Setting
Your Pricing

Y ou have a variety of options when it comes

to setting your rates, so this can be a tricky

and sometimes confusing process. Unless you're

offering unique higher-end services and have little compe-

tition, your rates need to be fair and consistent with your

competitors while still allowing you to earn a profit.

How much you charge your clients is based on ten key factors:

1. The services you'll be offering
2. Your education, previous experience, and proven successes performing your services
3. Any specialized training or certifications you possess that directly relate to the services you offer
4. The level of complexity of the services
5. The demand for your services
6. The types of clients you'll be catering to
7. What your competition charges
8. The perceived added value of working with you, based on the premium brand you create for yourself and your business
9. The financial investment you need to make as you're establishing your business
10. The ongoing monthly expenses required to keep your business operational, which need to be built into the rates you charge so you can cover your costs of doing business and generate a profit

> **tip** ⓘ
>
> Even if you have skills and experience that you've used for years as a full-time employee in the corporate world, until you've proved your worth to a client, you may need to keep your rates a bit lower at first. The trick, however, is never to undercharge based on what a client thinks you're worth and what your competition is charging to handle similar work.

As a rule, if you're handling routine, entry-level tasks for your clients, ones they'd typically pay an employee minimum wage to handle, you probably won't be able to charge much more than minimum wage for your services.

However, if you're handling tasks and projects that require a specialized skill set, as well as previous experience, you'll be able to charge significantly higher rates.

Unfortunately, there is no proven formula to use for setting your rates. A lot will depend on the research you do on the ten pricing factors listed above, and then on your ability to establish a positive relationship with your clients as you prove your value to them moving forward. You may need to experiment with your rates a bit as you establish your virtual assistant business. At first, refrain from publishing your rates online or in printed brochures, so you can negotiate with your initial clients.

Keep in mind, not all virtual assistants publicly display or advertise their rates. One approach some virtual assistants have successfully adopted is to get a potential client interested in your services, and then engage in a one-on-one discussion about their unique needs. After you determine how they could benefit from your services, you can then

tip

You may find it beneficial to offer a discounted, highly competitive "introductory rate" for your services. This could be a five- or ten-hour prepaid package, for example, that you only offer to new clients. After this, once you've proved yourself, you'll likely have little difficulty renewing your contract with the client at your standard rate.

provide them with a custom price quote, based on the type of business relationship you're both seeking.

Ultimately, above and beyond being able to cover your initial investment and operating costs, you need to feel you're being paid what you're worth to maintain a positive attitude over the long term. If, over time, you feel underpaid and underappreciated, you'll lose motivation, experience burnout, and start hating your work. This will lead to emotional and financial problems down the road.

The first step in setting your rates should be to crunch some numbers and figure out how much you need to earn per hour, per day, per week, and per month to cover all your business expenses and generate a profit you're satisfied with.

Second, do some research and determine the market value for the services you'll be offering. Start by learning as much as you can from your competition. Third, brainstorm how you can create a premium brand for yourself and your business, so you can justify charging premium rates.

First Calculate Your Initial Investment and Cost of Doing Business

It's essential to understand your cost of doing business and your initial financial investment before you set your rates. However much you wind up charging your clients, you need to cover these expenses, your own salary, and potentially generate a profit.

When launching your business, there will be some upfront, out-of-pocket expenses. You'll want to anticipate as many of these as possible, so you can budget for them before your virtual assistant business starts generating revenue.

warning

As you're setting your pricing, never believe you're worth more than you really are to your clients. It's important to be honest with yourself and be able to justify the rates you charge. Based on the ten pricing factors mentioned, be realistic in terms of your current earning potential and value. Moving forward, figure out how you can enhance your skill set, expand your service offerings, and make yourself more valuable to your clients in the future.

▶ Understand Who Your Competition Actually Is

When analyzing your competition, focus on other virtual assistants in your city, state, and country—not on what VAs in other countries are charging. Don't consider someone in another time zone, who is not proficient in your native language (or the native language spoken by your prospective clients), and who charges 10 or 20 cents on the dollar compared to VAs in your country to be your competition.

Companies who have worked with virtual assistants understand the saying "You get what you pay for," and many have learned firsthand that working with a very low-cost virtual assistant from another country often leads to scheduling and communication problems, quality issues, miscommunications, and language barriers.

Also determine what it would cost a potential client to hire a part-time or full-time employee to handle the tasks you'd be doing and try to calculate how much they would save by working with an independent contractor like you. This can help you justify your rates.

Once your business is operational, you'll incur a wide range of fixed and variable expenses. It's essential to keep detailed records (preferably using bookkeeping software) and maintain an accurate understanding of how much money you need to spend for your business to function. (These are your operating expenses.)

Making an Initial Investment in Your Business

The worksheet in Figure 5–1 on page 75 will help you determine what you need to start your virtual assistant business and calculate your initial financial investment. Based on the niche you plan to cater to, or the specific services you plan to provide your clients, additional software, tools, and equipment may be required.

Ongoing Fixed and Variable Business Expenses

To get your business off the ground and maintain its day-to-day operation, there will be ongoing expenses (both fixed and variable costs) that you'll need to cover.

You'll want to calculate and budget for these potential ongoing expenses right away:

▶ Accounting/bookkeeping/tax preparation services
▶ Advertising
▶ Business insurance

Initial Investment Worksheet

Equipment	Description	Currently Own	Immediately Need	Future Investment	Cost
Accounting and/or Legal Services		❏ Yes ❏ No	❏ Yes ❏ No	❏ Yes ❏ No	$
Additional Office Equipment		❏ Yes ❏ No	❏ Yes ❏ No	❏ Yes ❏ No	$
Bookkeeping Software		❏ Yes ❏ No	❏ Yes ❏ No	❏ Yes ❏ No	$
Branding-Related Costs (Logo Design, etc.)		❏ Yes ❏ No	❏ Yes ❏ No	❏ Yes ❏ No	$
Business Software		❏ Yes ❏ No	❏ Yes ❏ No	❏ Yes ❏ No	$
Desk		❏ Yes ❏ No	❏ Yes ❏ No	❏ Yes ❏ No	$
Desk Chair		❏ Yes ❏ No	❏ Yes ❏ No	❏ Yes ❏ No	$
Desktop Computer		❏ Yes ❏ No	❏ Yes ❏ No	❏ Yes ❏ No	$
High-Capacity External Hard Drive		❏ Yes ❏ No	❏ Yes ❏ No	❏ Yes ❏ No	$
Landline Phone		❏ Yes ❏ No	❏ Yes ❏ No	❏ Yes ❏ No	$
Laptop Computer		❏ Yes ❏ No	❏ Yes ❏ No	❏ Yes ❏ No	$

FIGURE 5-1: **Initial Investment Worksheet**

Initial Investment Worksheet

Equipment	Description	Currently Own	Immediately Need	Future Investment	Cost
Letterhead, Business Cards, Printed Brochures, etc.		❑ Yes ❑ No	❑ Yes ❑ No	❑ Yes ❑ No	$
Office Supplies		❑ Yes ❑ No	❑ Yes ❑ No	❑ Yes ❑ No	$
Other Specialty Software		❑ Yes ❑ No	❑ Yes ❑ No	❑ Yes ❑ No	$
Phone Service (Including Call Management Services)		❑ Yes ❑ No	❑ Yes ❑ No	❑ Yes ❑ No	$
Printer/ Scanner/ Copier (Combo)		❑ Yes ❑ No	❑ Yes ❑ No	❑ Yes ❑ No	$
Smartphone		❑ Yes ❑ No	❑ Yes ❑ No	❑ Yes ❑ No	$
Storage & Filing Cabinets		❑ Yes ❑ No	❑ Yes ❑ No	❑ Yes ❑ No	$
Tablet		❑ Yes ❑ No	❑ Yes ❑ No	❑ Yes ❑ No	$
Website Creation and Hosting		❑ Yes ❑ No	❑ Yes ❑ No	❑ Yes ❑ No	$
Other					$
Other					$

FIGURE 5–1: **Initial Investment Worksheet,** continued

- ▶ Business software, online collaboration and communications tools, and related online service subscriptions
- ▶ Health insurance
- ▶ Internet service
- ▶ Legal services
- ▶ Marketing
- ▶ Office and printing supplies
- ▶ Paid advertising
- ▶ Payment (credit card) processing fees
- ▶ Phone service
- ▶ Promotional expenses
- ▶ Public relations
- ▶ Social media activities
- ▶ Taxes
- ▶ Website maintenance and content creation

> **tip** ⓘ
>
> Assuming you'll be working from home, you'll want to allocate a portion of your home's utility bills, rent/mortgage expenses, and car expenses, for example, as business expenses for tax purposes. Be sure to speak with your accountant about this so you can claim the appropriate deductions.

Financial Management

It's important to monitor your financial progress closely, and the only way you can do that is by keeping detailed records. You can handle the process manually; however, there are several excellent bookkeeping and accounting applications you can use. For example, there's Intuit's QuickBooks (https://quickbooks.intuit.com/) and Oracle's NetSuite (https://www.netsuite.com/portal/home.shtml), which are the leading accounting and bookkeeping applications used by small businesses. A few other options include FreshBooks (https://www.freshbooks.com/), Wave (https://www.waveapps.com/), and Zoho Books (https://www.zoho.com/us/books/).

Whatever accounting/bookkeeping system you use will help you produce financial statements that tell you exactly where you stand and what you need to do next. The key financial statements you need to understand and use regularly are:

- ▶ *P&L statement* (also called the income statement). This statement illustrates how much your virtual assistant business is making or losing over a designated period—monthly, quarterly, or annually—by subtracting expenses from your revenue to arrive at a net result, which is either a profit or a loss. Initially, this document may not be of much value to you—especially during the startup phase. But as your profit history grows, you will appreciate this useful financial management statement.

▶ *Balance sheet.* A balance sheet is a table showing your assets, liabilities, and capital at a specific point in time. A balance sheet is typically generated monthly, quarterly, or annually when the business's books are closed.

▶ *Cash-flow statement.* This summarizes the operating, investing, and financing activities of your business as they relate to the inflow and outflow of cash. Its main purpose is to point out when the cash flow isn't flowing so you can work out a solution and pinpoint trouble spots in the future. As with the P&L statement, a cash-flow statement is prepared to reflect a specific accounting period, such as monthly, quarterly, or annually.

Successful business owners review these reports at least monthly, so they always know where they stand and can quickly act to correct minor difficulties before they become major financial problems. If you wait until June to figure out whether you made a profit last December, you will not be in business very long.

Once you have a fiscal system in place, your next step should be to open a separate checking account for your

> **warning** ⚠
>
> Especially during the startup phase, try to avoid using your personal or company credit card(s) to cover business expenses, unless you have the funds to pay off your credit card balances at the end of each month. If you rack up a high credit card balance, this will negatively impact your credit rating and result in high monthly interest fees. If your business goes bust for whatever reason, you will likely be held personally responsible for its credit card bills.

▶ Choose the Best Credit Card(s) for Your Business

If you carry a balance on a credit card that is used solely for business purposes, the interest is deductible, but if you mix business and personal charges on the card, the interest is not even partially deductible. Consult with your accountant to learn more about possible credit card interest deductions before filing your taxes.

When choosing which credit card(s) to acquire for your business, pay attention to its perks, like cash back or the ability to earn frequent flier miles. Choose a card with no annual fees, a competitive interest rate, and perks you'll benefit from. The CreditCards.com website (https://www.creditcards.com/) offers a free online tool to help you find the best credit card deals you'd qualify for, based on your creditworthiness.

business so that you don't commingle personal and business funds. You will also need at least one business credit card, or at least a separate credit card in your name that you use exclusively for your business.

Tax Matters

Your business is required to pay a variety of local, state, and federal taxes. Make sure you keep detailed and accurate records so you can deduct the expenses of operating your business. Making a mistake on your taxes can be costly when you consider the penalties and interest charges you could incur.

If you have employees, you'll be responsible for payroll taxes. Even if you are self-employed with no employees, you'll still need to pay the self-employment tax (which goes toward Social Security and Medicare).

You must report *all income* from your business, no matter how insignificant. Failing to do so is a crime! If the IRS starts poring over your financial records, the defense of "Oops, I didn't know I needed to pay taxes on business revenue" or "I didn't think you would catch me" won't get you very far. Make sure you review all your tax liabilities with an accountant.

Of course, in addition to reporting all your income, you should take every single deduction to which you are legally entitled. Homebased businesses may qualify for the home office deduction, which allows you to deduct a portion of your rent, mortgage interest, household utilities and services, real estate taxes, homeowner's insurance, repairs, security systems, and depreciation. If you're regularly driving back and forth to the post office, go on other business-related errands, or drive yourself to specific locations as part of your work for clients, you can either deduct mileage or depreciate your car and write off the actual expenses.

How Will You Get Paid?

An important part of financial management is setting up an easy-to-maintain accounts receivable system. This includes establishing clear and appropriate policies that are fair to your clients while protecting you.

As part of their billing practices, some virtual assistants extend credit to their clients by systematically

tip

Use your printed invoices as a marketing tool. Add a brochure or promotional flier into the envelope before mailing it out. Even though the invoice is going to an existing client, you never know where your brochures will end up, and you should always strive to earn repeat business and referrals from existing customers. Also include a services menu inside your brochure. An existing client might discover they'd benefit from using you for additional tasks.

generating invoices or monthly statements. This task can be easily handled with bookkeeping software, like QuickBooks, that includes an invoicing module. Many of the specialty applications designed for virtual assistants, such as Adminja and HoneyBook, include modules for handling time tracking and invoice generation, which then sync financial data with your bookkeeping software.

If you choose to design your own invoices and statements (for branding purposes), be sure they're clear and easy to understand. Detail each item and indicate the amount due in bold, with the words "Amount Due" in front of the total. A confusing invoice may be set aside for clarification, delaying payment.

If you're not being paid upfront by your clients, decide when payments are due and make that a clear part of your policy statement and contract with each client. Your policy should also address how far an account can go into arrears before you suspend services to that client or turn over the debt to a collection agency. This is always a tough call, but remember that you are a for-profit business, and if you don't get paid, you can't pay your own bills.

> **tip** ⓘ
>
> In your contract, include a statement describing which methods of payment (cash, credit cards, checks, and/or electronic payment services) you accept. This will depend on the credit card merchant account provider or financial institution you work with. Many website hosting services and bookkeeping software publishers offer an ecommerce/digital payments solution that will include handling credit card, debit card, and electronic payment service (such as PayPal or Apple Pay) transactions.

Accepting Credit and Debit Cards

Whether for convenience, security, reward points, or out of habit, many of your clients (especially if they operate a small business themselves) will prefer to pay for your work with a credit card. Most virtual assistants find accepting credit and debit cards is a plus. Fortunately, it's much easier to get merchant status now than in the past; in fact, these days merchant account providers are competing aggressively for your business.

To get a credit card merchant account, you no longer need to start with your own bank. Shop around! It's worth taking the time to get the best deal.

Services like Square (https://squareup.com/), PayPal (https://www.paypal.com/), and Intuit (https://quickbooks.intuit.com/payments) provide easy-to-set-up merchant account services with no long-term contracts. They charge competitive fees only when you use the service to collect payments. These merchant account services are typically compatible with the ecommerce components of most turnkey website services. If you want clients to purchase your time through your website, make sure this is compatible with both your merchant account provider and website hosting service.

Accepting Checks

Although paying by plastic is popular, many of your clients may prefer to write you a check. Businesses lose billions of dollars annually due to bad checks, so look for these key points when accepting them:

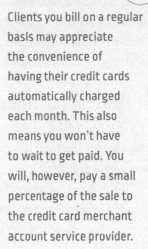

aha!

Clients you bill on a regular basis may appreciate the convenience of having their credit cards automatically charged each month. This also means you won't have to wait to get paid. You will, however, pay a small percentage of the sale to the credit card merchant account service provider.

- ▶ Check the date. Do not accept a check that is undated, postdated, or more than 30 days old.
- ▶ Be sure the written amount and numerical amount agree.
- ▶ If applicable, make sure the check is signed by an authorized signatory.
- ▶ All information on the check, including the bank's routing number, the client's checking account number, the check number, the name of the company, and the amount of the check, is all clearly legible.
- ▶ Don't accept temporary checks from startup clients. The paper check should have the client's name and all relevant information preprinted on it.

Include your check acceptance policies in your contract. It should spell out the steps you will take (and the fees you will charge) if you must return a check for nonpayment. Most clients understand the risks you take when accepting checks and will be willing to follow your rules.

If most of your clients are local and you're providing services in a middle-income or high-income area, the risk associated with accepting checks is much lower. You always have the option, however, of initiating a "No personal checks accepted" policy, especially when dealing with not-yet-funded startups or one-person businesses.

What's in the Financial Forecast?

You don't need a crystal ball to predict future revenue, but you do need a formula to foresee how much you can expect to make in the weeks, months, and years ahead.

Pay close attention to and use your key financial statements on a routine basis. Plan for the costs of growth and watch for signs of developing problems so you can figure out how to best deal with them before they turn into a major crisis. Honing your analytical foresight demonstrates that you are an astute business owner on top of every situation.

Common Pricing Options Used by Virtual Assistants

As you already know, how much you charge your clients should be based on a range of criteria, not an arbitrary and unjustifiable decision. There are a few pricing models that VAs typically use, although some VAs create a hybrid pricing model that works for them and appeals more to their clients.

Get Paid by the Hour

In this model, you set a flat hourly rate and then charge your clients as you go or send them an invoice for the total hours you've worked at the end of your predetermined billing cycle (a week or a month).

This is good for your clients because they can use as much or as little of your time as they need, whenever they need it, with no upfront costs and zero long-term obligation. The downside for you as the VA is that it'll be hard to plan your schedule because from week to week, you won't know each client's needs. You also run the risk (albeit small) of not getting paid after you've done the work.

This pricing option works if you're not looking to develop long-term relationships with your clients and don't mind getting hired on an as-needed basis for specific projects or tasks.

Offer Prepaid Packages

This pricing option involves you promoting your standard hourly rate, and then offering a discount based on how many hours of your time a client commits to. Different package options might include:

▶ 5 hours per week (or month) with a 3 percent discount off your fixed hourly rate when paid in advance

▶ 10 hours per week (or month) with a 5 percent discount off your fixed hourly rate when paid in advance

▶ 20 hours per week (or month) with an 8 percent discount off your fixed hourly rate when paid in advance

▶ 25 hours or more per week (or month) with a 10 percent discount off your fixed hourly rate when paid in advance

tip

Even though your clients will be signing a written contract with you before you start working for them, especially if you'll be working with not-yet fully funded startups, you should protect your financial interests by requesting at least half of what you'll be charging upfront and the other half upon completion of the work you've been hired to do.

If you adopt this pricing model, you must decide whether to allow your clients to bank unused hours and roll them over to the next week (or month), or if unused time expires at the end of each given time period with no refunds issued. The pricing model used by VAs is a matter of personal preference and can even be done on a client-by-client basis, based on the relationship you have with a particular client. By allowing your prepaid time to expire, it encourages clients to use your services in a timely manner, and then potentially renew your contract.

Some virtual assistants also require their clients to pay for a minimum number of hours per week (or month) over a minimum period of weeks (or months) to receive a larger discount—thus committing to a longer-term relationship with you.

For example, you might require your client to sign a three-month-long retainer that includes at least ten hours per week of your time. If a client prepays for a block of time, say 10, 20, 30, or 40 hours in a week or month, you might offer them between 5 and 25 percent off your published hourly rate.

The benefit to your client is that they're virtually guaranteed access to you when they need it. And knowing that they have paid for your time in advance, they'll be more inclined to rely on you, perhaps for a broader range of tasks. For you, this pricing model works well

▶ Your Hourly Rate Might Vary by Service

Some virtual assistants have a niche or specialty, but within their area of expertise, they offer a variety of services. If you're one of them, it might be wise (and more lucrative) for you to set different hourly rates depending on the service(s) you'll be performing for each client.

For example, if your specialty is online marketing, you might charge $30 per hour to handle a client's social media feeds, but you might raise your rates to $50 per hour to create and implement an email marketing campaign.

If you're asked to create a series of blog posts, you might charge $40 per post (not per hour), and to write a press release for a company, you might charge a flat fee of $300. (These rates are for demonstration purposes only, and do not reflect suggested pricing for these services.)

Charging different prices for different services works well if your pricing structure is easy for the client to understand. Make sure your services menu clearly indicates how much you charge for each service, and repeat the information in your contract. To keep things simple, only list charges in your contract for services you will be performing for the client. If their needs expand, you can always update the contract.

because you're paid in advance, and you know from week to week or month to month how much time you'll need to allocate to each of your clients.

Charge a Retainer and Then a Discounted Hourly Rate

This pricing model basically involves the client hiring you for a guaranteed number of hours per week or month, but if they go beyond that time allocation, they pay a discounted hourly rate for that extra time.

If your usual rate is $50 per hour, a retainer might be for a minimum of ten hours per week (at a discounted rate of $47.50 per hour), with a four-week commitment. Any additional time beyond that would be billed at $45 per hour. The client would prepay for a week (or a month), but at the end of that period, they would receive an invoice for any extra hours they used.

Charge a Pre-Negotiated Flat Fee for Each Project

Instead of charging a client by the hour to complete their tasks or projects, you would negotiate a flat fee for each task or project, regardless of how long it takes you to complete it. For some specialized types of services, this model might make more sense for you, because you're basing your rate more on your skills and expertise, as opposed to your time.

For example, if you are a writer and a client asks you to produce a 1,500-word article for their website, that might take you just two hours, but the going rate for that type of content is $300. If you charged them your standard hourly rate of $50, you'd only earn $100 for that task, but if you charged a flat fee of $300, you'd make $150 per hour! On the other hand, if the process takes longer than anticipated and you wind up spending five hours researching and writing the article, you would lose money accepting a flat rate.

From the client's perspective, if the project requirements are spelled out in detail, they can budget for it, knowing exactly what it will cost upfront. They won't have to wait until you're finished to determine how many hours you spent on it.

If you're hired through an online service such as Upwork or Fiverr (which you'll learn more about in Chapter 6), those clients tend to prefer paying a flat rate per project and will only hire a VA on a per-project basis. You likely won't have the opportunity to develop a long-term and potentially lucrative relationship with clients from those sites. Thus, more of your ongoing efforts (and time) will be dedicated to finding and landing new clients.

More Strategies for Setting Your Rates

Many of the experienced virtual assistants interviewed for this book offered specific tips for setting rates, based on their own experiences. While you'll learn more about these VAs in

Chapter 9, here's what some of them had to say about setting your rates and the best way to be paid by clients.

Amy Foley, cofounder of Inbound Back Office, said, "When a potential client tells me they can hire someone from overseas for a lot less money than what my agency charges, I simply encourage them to try that route if they are that cost-conscious. I then warn them that they'll likely encounter communication issues. If the client tries to explain a complex task to a foreign VA, it will not be received or understood as easily for someone when English is not their native language."

Foley added, "When I was first starting out as a virtual assistant, I charged an hourly rate. I then doubled it when I started working with my business coach, who became my mentor. I was surprised that I still landed new clients after that dramatic rate hike. A lot of times when you set your rates, if someone believes your rates are too low, in their mind they'll think there's a catch or that they'll wind up getting poor-quality results. I believe it's important to know your worth as a virtual assistant and be able to back up your price by offering superior work. Based on my own experience, I have found that it's helpful to keep your pricing model very simple when you're selling yourself and onboarding clients. I no longer offer packages because there is too much gray area. People want rates that are easy to understand and budget for."

When it comes to billing clients and getting paid, early in her career Foley sold hourly blocks of time, which she had her clients pay for upfront. "I offered five- and ten-hour blocks," she said. "The more hours a client purchased, the lower the hourly rate was, which was their incentive to purchase more and larger blocks of hours. I listed my prices for different blocks of time on my website and allowed clients to prepay for what they wanted using the Stripe payment method, which was integrated into the website. I then tracked my time using Toggl and kept the client apprised of their available time. When their block of time was running out, I asked them if they wanted to prepurchase another block of hours. I kept really detailed records as well as did accurate tracking of my time."

She recalls that in her early days, she never had any problem getting her clients to prepay for her time, although new clients sometimes purchased a very small block of hours to try her out before making a large commitment. "If you don't have an established reputation and existing clients who will vouch for you with potential new clients, offering a small block of time requires a minimal financial commitment and eliminates the risk for the company or individual hiring you," she said.

David Hogan, who is now a virtual assistant after spending 17 years working in executive support in the corporate world, explained how he determined his initial rates: "I had a friend who was already serving as a virtual assistant. He shared the rates he was charging and what was working well for him. When I started as a VA, I tested those rates with my early clients to see how they reacted, and I did some number crunching on my own to calculate the rates I needed to charge to sustain my business. Based on my experience and skill set back then, I was able to charge between $40 and $50 per hour. I knew I could not afford to charge less than $40 per hour."

During his initial discussions with potential clients, Hogan went over the types of projects and tasks he could accomplish for each client, and then asked them point-blank what they were willing to pay for those services.

"This got the conversation about rates started. These days, I offer discounted long-term packages to clients, with my base rate being $45 per hour. I offer a 20-, 40-, and 80-hour per month package. During the conversation, I will ask specifically what the client is trying to get done, so I can offer them realistic expectations about how long their tasks or projects will take. All of my packages are offered on a month-to-month, prepaid basis, with no long-term commitment," said Hogan.

He added, "I like to keep my pricing simple. The clients, especially if they're a startup, appreciate not having to make a long-term commitment. When I am dealing with a startup, I do as much research about them as possible before the onboarding process to make sure they have the funding in place to afford and ultimately pay me for my services. Once I develop a relationship with a startup company, I have had several wanting to pay me one year in advance for my services, based on a 40-hour-per-month package, once they were fully funded."

Since 2016, Molly Morgan has been an independent virtual assistant who specializes in digital marketing. She explained, "Initially I went off a few things when setting my rates, starting with a calculation of how much I wanted and needed to be earning per hour. I then researched my value in the marketplace based on my skill set and experience. I had previously worked for a marketing agency and handled digital marketing. Initially, I offered packages based on an hourly rate, which averaged about $50 per hour."

After starting to work with a business coach who served as her mentor, Morgan stated that these days, she creates pricing based on the specific services she will be performing for a client and the deliverables they're requesting. "When I create an email marketing package, for example, I list out all the deliverables they will be receiving and set my price based on those specific services, not the amount of time it will take me to complete the task or project," she said.

For virtual assistants who are just starting out and are using an online service such as Upwork or Fiverr to find and land clients, Morgan stated that in her experience, companies using these services are typically looking for a VA to complete a single task. They're not looking to build a long-term relationship. "These days, when I begin working with a new client, I insist that they commit to a minimum of a three-month retainer. I no longer spend the time and energy trying to land very short-term clients," said Morgan, who does all her billing, invoicing, and payment processing with the HoneyBook software for virtual assistants. She herself has hired a virtual assistant to handle her client billing.

Once a client has committed to a three-month retainer for Morgan's digital marketing services, each month she requires 50 percent of that month's payment upfront, with the other 50 percent due two weeks later. This payment schedule continues for the entire retainer period.

Vickie Hadge, owner of Virtually Done by Vickie, is an independent virtual assistant who has been in business since 2003. When she first needed to set her rates, she solicited advice from the members of the virtual assistant networking group she was part of. "One mistake that I believe a lot of virtual assistants make is that they undervalue themselves," she said. "They set their rates as if they're working full time in an office for a single employer. What these people don't factor in are their operating costs and expenses. I send out invoices once per month to my clients, who have already signed a contract with me that outlines my rates and when I get paid."

Erin Dahlquist is a virtual assistant who works with an agency that matches up her strengths and capabilities with what the agency's clients are looking for. Thus she does not have to find her own clients or set her own rates. She previously worked full time as a marketing professional for a sporting goods company.

When asked if she could make more money being an independent virtual assistant, Dahlquist replied, "If I wanted to work full time as a VA, I would definitely want to be independent. Since I choose to work part time doing this, I am willing to be paid less and not have the added responsibility of running a VA business. I know I could double my hourly rate as an independent VA, but that would add the extra burden and responsibilities that I don't want. The agency sets my rates, but if I were doing this myself, I would call a bunch of VAs offering similar services, find out what they charge, and use that as a guideline for setting my own rates."

fun fact ☺

The Association of Virtual Assistants (https://associationofvas.com/) has published a report, called "Your Guide to Industry Standard Virtual Assistant Pricing," that you can download for free. This informative report will help you set your prices based on what clients are expecting to pay.

You Won't Land Any Clients Without Marketing, Advertising, and Promoting Your Business

As you can see, the rates VAs charge, and how they're paid, are based on multiple factors. Each virtual assistant must develop their own strategy for setting their rates, and these strategies tend to evolve over time as clients' demands change and your experience and skill set expand.

However, unless you do a stellar job marketing, advertising, and promoting your business on an ongoing basis, you won't have any clients. And without clients, you have no income.

The next chapter focuses on ways to market, advertise, and promote your virtual assistant business, both online and in the real world. As you'll discover, networking and word-of-mouth advertising are very affordable and will likely generate the best results when it comes to finding and landing new clients.

Marketing Your Business to Find Clients

I n the film *Field of Dreams*, Kevin Costner's character famously heard a mysterious voice in his cornfield say, "If you build it, he will come." In his case, it meant a baseball field. However, building and then launching your virtual assistant business is only the first step toward achieving success. You still have a lot of work to do!

Once you've set up a firm foundation for your VA business and you're ready to take on clients, take a moment to congratulate yourself. You've already come a lot further than many people ever do.

Now figure out how many hours per week you're available to work on behalf of your clients. Is this a side hustle you're willing to dedicate 10 hours to, a part-time job you can allocate 20 hours to, or do you hope it will become a full-time (40+ hours per week) job?

Regardless of your answer to these questions, in addition to the hours you spend working with your paying clients, you'll need to dedicate time to operating and managing your business, during which time you'll handle things like bookkeeping, marketing, promotions, sales, and networking—tasks that are essential, but which you do not get directly paid for.

From this point forward, and on an ongoing basis, you need to attract a steady flow of paying clients. Some of the strategies that will help you accomplish this are free. Others typically work well but require at least some (upfront) financial investment. All require your time to properly implement.

warning

No matter how many hours per week you plan to dedicate to your virtual assistant business, remember that some of those hours will be spent managing your business (which you don't get paid for), as opposed to the work you'll be doing for your clients (which you do get paid for).

One of those management tasks is to continuously seek out and land new clients. Make sure you block out an ample amount of time in your schedule for this essential task, or you'll quickly find yourself with few or no paying clients.

tip

One way to save some time is to hire your own virtual assistant to handle your company's social media marketing and/or website management, for example. A VA with a background in marketing and online advertising can help you promote your business and save you from having to master these skills yourself.

So unless you get lucky and immediately land enough paying clients to fill your entire schedule, and each client commits to a long-term contract, you will need to maintain your advertising, marketing, promotional, and networking efforts on an ongoing basis to attract a steady flow of paying clients. This is time you are not paid for, but it still needs to be allocated, along with the cost of implementing these strategies.

When choosing how to promote, market, and advertise your VA business, adopt a multifaceted approach. In other words, pick at least three different strategies, and use them simultaneously and on an ongoing basis. Every one to three months, evaluate the success of each approach and then either tweak your strategy or try something altogether different.

Let's focus on some of the ways successful virtual assistants find new client prospects.

A Social Media Presence Is a Must

Creating and maintaining a presence for your business on social media is essential. Initially, you'll want to create a Facebook page for your business (which is separate from your personal page), and establish a presence for yourself and your business on LinkedIn.

The purpose of maintaining a branded company page on these two platforms is to promote your business directly to potential customers, educate others about what you do, and establish an informal way to communicate with prospective clients (and the public). Doing this will allow you to position yourself as an expert in your field, someone with specialized skills and experience. It'll also allow you to create a virtual community of people who might be interested in your services.

The core reason for maintaining a company page on these two services is to share information and establish connections, while directing interested parties to your company website or encouraging them to call you directly for a free consultation.

tip

To create a branded Facebook page for your business (for free), visit Facebook for Business (www.facebook.com/).

To establish a personal LinkedIn account, visit https://www.linkedin.com/; to establish a LinkedIn page for your business, visit LinkedIn Pages (https://business.linkedin.com/).

Through your company's Facebook and LinkedIn pages, you can foster engagement by sharing photos, articles, PowerPoint presentations, PDFs, Word documents, videos, and other content that will help you tell your story and provide valuable information or advice to your potential clients. These social media platforms can also help you establish and build your brand in a way that specifically targets your intended audience.

By first determining your niche and then clarifying which types of clients you want to attract (and in what industries), you should then get to know their social media habits and establish a presence on the other social media services they are active on, such as Twitter, Instagram, Pinterest, and/or TikTok.

The key to a successful social media presence is to provide valuable and useful information to your audience, for free, and on a consistent basis. Someone who visits your page may not be looking for a virtual assistant at that moment, but by encouraging ongoing engagement and repeat visits to your page, when they do need a VA, you'll be at the top of their list.

Use social media to showcase your skills, experience, and unique talents in ways your potential clients could benefit from. Use your content to educate them about how their organization could use a virtual assistant, and focus on catering to the interests, wants, needs, problems, and financial challenges your potential clients may be facing.

When creating the profile and overview for your Facebook and LinkedIn pages, you'll have the opportunity to showcase your company's logo, create a searchable description of your business, publish your own bio, prominently display your contact information (including your website URL), and create a list of keywords that people can use to find your business when they're searching Facebook or LinkedIn.

Most important, your Facebook and LinkedIn pages, along with the content you publish on those pages, should include a call to action. In other words, encourage people to visit your website, call you directly to learn more about your company, or hire you as their new virtual assistant.

In addition to the keywords used to describe your Facebook or LinkedIn page, be sure to add hashtags (#Keywords) to your posts, which allow users to find your content more easily. As you create your content, focus on ways you can capture the attention of your intended audience with your posts. Creatively using relevant photos and graphics in conjunction with text is one powerful way to do this.

There are a wide range of low-cost stock photography services that make finding eye-catching photos and graphics easy. Check out iStock (https://www.istockphoto.com/), Shutterstock (https://www.shutterstock.com/), or Adobe Stock (https://stock.adobe.com), for example.

Using a bit of creativity and your own expertise in your specialty, use your presence on Facebook and LinkedIn to:

---

fun fact ☺

Other calls to action you should use on social media include encouraging people to follow/subscribe to your page, "like" specific posts, comment on posts, and share posts with their friends. LinkedIn offers an action plan to help small businesses maximize engagement on their site: https://business.linkedin.com/marketing-solutions/linkedin-pages/for-small-business.

Keep in mind that company pages with completed profiles that show a lot of user engagement tend to attract the most initial and repeat visitors, followers, and subscribers.

- ▶ Attract potential new clients
- ▶ Share free information and advice
- ▶ Answer commonly asked questions related to your business, VAs in general, or your area of expertise
- ▶ Describe your business and the unique collection of services it offers

▶ There Are Multiple Ways to Use Facebook and LinkedIn

On both Facebook and LinkedIn, you'll want to create a free personal page for yourself and a separate page for your virtual assistant business. However, another powerful way to take advantage of these services is to use paid advertising to target very specific people and guide them to your business page and company website.

To learn about the advertising opportunities for small businesses on Facebook, visit https://www.facebook.com/business/ads; to learn about similar opportunities on LinkedIn, visit https://business.linkedin.com/marketing-solutions/ads. You can launch an online campaign for as little as $50 and use the tools offered by these services to ensure only your target audience will see the ads.

On Facebook, another powerful free marketing strategy is to join and become active on Facebook groups. Hundreds of thousands of unique Facebook groups cater to people with specific interests or occupations. Start by joining groups related to small business and virtual assistants, and then expand your activities by joining groups related to the specialized services you offer and the specific industries you cater to.

Engage on these groups by sharing how-to advice, answering questions posted by other people, responding to content and comments posted by others, and networking (informally) with people you identify as prospective clients.

To find Facebook groups to join, log in to Facebook from either your personal or business page, and enter a keyword related to an area of interest in the search field. Facebook also offers a special search tool for finding and joining Facebook groups, which you can find at https://www.facebook.com/groups/discover.

Becoming active on special interest Facebook groups allows you to casually promote yourself and your company while interacting with other people who might be prospective clients. Yes, becoming active on multiple Facebook groups can be time-consuming, but it's free. It's a viable option, especially if you're on a tight budget.

- ▶ Compose and publish articles and posts about how clients can hire you as a virtual assistant to save themselves time and money, or to overcome challenges they're currently facing
- ▶ Share your expert insight into specific topics related to the services you offer or the industry you cater to
- ▶ Promote online-only discounts to your followers and subscribers
- ▶ Share recommendations from your existing clients
- ▶ Interact informally with potential clients
- ▶ Learn more about the needs and concerns of prospective clients
- ▶ Share links to interesting articles or videos you've come across elsewhere on the internet
- ▶ Demonstrate and showcase ways you differentiate yourself from your competition, focusing on why this should appeal to prospective clients

Another option is to use YouTube as a business marketing tool. For this to work, you'll need to produce a series of informational videos that you publish on your company's branded YouTube channel. Creating and managing the YouTube channel is free, but depending on the approach you take, it can be costly to produce a series of professional-quality videos.

▶ Learn More About It!

Entrepreneur Press (https://shop.aer.io/EntrepreneurBooks) publishes an entire collection of how-to books targeted to small business owners interested in using social media and the internet (including email) as a powerful marketing, sales, and promotional tool.

Be sure to take advantage of these information-packed, low-cost resources. You'll also find online courses, adult education classes, and other professional development programs that can help you enhance your social media and internet marketing skills.

For example, check out the online courses available from:

- ▶ Coursera: https://www.coursera.org/
- ▶ Digital Marketing Institute: https://digitalmarketinginstitute.com
- ▶ Freelance University: https://www.freelanceu.com
- ▶ LinkedIn Small Business Marketing: https://www.linkedin.com/
- ▶ Skye Learning: https://skyelearning.com
- ▶ Udemy: https://www.udemy.com

Of course, you can also showcase your informational, demonstration, or how-to videos on your company's website, but one of the benefits of publishing them on YouTube is that each video will quickly get listed on Google as well as YouTube, making it easier for potential clients to discover your company.

Each video should have a clear call to action that sends people to your company's website or encourages them to call you directly.

Email and/or Direct-Mail Marketing

When promoting your virtual assistant business, consider reaching out to your circle of friends and acquaintances, as well as past customers, clients, and online followers through personalized email to tell them about your new business venture, offer your services, and ask them to provide referrals for you. Remember, there's a big difference between using personalized email to reach out to people you know (and who know you) and sending spam.

Spam refers to unsolicited email that's not wanted by the recipients. Spam is often associated with scams; you should avoid it, since the response rate will be low, and it will tarnish your company's reputation.

For people you know, who know you, and/or who have opted into your email list, email marketing allows you to compose and send personalized emails to select groups of people, and target your message accordingly. By using email marketing tools, you can create separate databases with contact details for focused groups of people, and then target each group with a different set of carefully composed email messages.

So as you're gearing up to launch, be sure to reach out to your inner circle via email to tell them about your new business and personally ask for their assistance.

As your company grows, use personalized emails to stay in touch with potential, current, and past clients and keep them updated on news about your business and the services you offer.

Create a group of email list databases pulled from your master email list and compose separate messages for different audiences. Some of the separate email list databases you might create and manage include:

tip

The *Ultimate Guide to YouTube for Business, 2nd Edition* by Jason R. Rich is published by Entrepreneur Press and covers all the ways you can create professional-quality videos on a tight budget and then attract a highly targeted audience for that content by using catchy, descriptive video titles, keywords, and other tools offered by YouTube and third parties.

- ▶ People in your inner circle
- ▶ Friends and acquaintances from the real world
- ▶ Customers, clients, followers, and other individuals who know you online, but not IRL (in real life)
- ▶ People who learned about your company from other promotional activities, including social media, and then opted into your email list (meaning they gave you their email address and permission to contact them)
- ▶ Past clients you'd like to do business with again
- ▶ Potential clients who have expressed an interest in your company
- ▶ Current clients who could benefit from expanding the ways they're using your services

By using email marketing software, it's easy to create and manage as many separate email lists as you need. You can write messages ahead of time that will be personalized to the intended recipients and sent whenever you wish.

Each email should contain at least one powerful call to action and explain how and why the reader will benefit from responding right away. For example: "Call [phone number] to schedule your free consultation within the next three days to receive a 15 percent discount off our most popular services for the length of your first contract."

The following strategies will help you write effective emails:

- ▶ Make sure each message is targeted specifically to its intended audience.
- ▶ Don't write your emails to a "target audience," though. Write each message as if you were sending it to just one person.
- ▶ Compose each message's subject line to capture the reader's attention right away. Don't try to be too clever, though. The message should look like a personal email, not a sales solicitation or spam.
- ▶ Use powerful, upbeat vocabulary that your target audience will understand and relate to. Keep the messaging simple. The SmartBlogger website has a useful article listing more than 801 "power words" that can be highly effective in a marketing email (https://smartblogger.com/power-words/).
- ▶ Keep your emails short, and get directly to the point. The overall length should be just a few paragraphs, and each paragraph should be no longer than two or three sentences. Don't waste the reader's time.
- ▶ Focus the content on the benefits of your services and how your company can help the reader.
- ▶ The tone should be friendly, upbeat, and personal. Avoid the hard sell. Instead, provide just enough information about your company to get the reader excited, so they'll want to visit your company's website to learn more.

► Include a call to action, and make it very easy to follow. Tell the reader exactly what they need to do next and why. Create a sense of urgency.

► As you're compiling your email list, make sure you spell everyone's name correctly. If you're using a prefix (Mr./Mrs./Ms./Dr.), make certain it's the appropriate one. It's also important that you fill in the fields in your email database correctly (such as First Name and Last Name), so that the salutations in your personalized emails are consistently accurate.

► Don't send out more than one email per week to each recipient. Make it clear that you won't be bombarding them with emails and you won't be sharing their contact information with other organizations. Respect the privacy of the people on your lists.

► Embed your logo into your emails. This will help you build your brand and convey a more professional image. Include an attractive email signature at the end of each email with your phone number, email address, website URL, and social media usernames.

► Proofread your outgoing emails carefully. Spelling mistakes, incorrect punctuation, or the incorrect use of words will immediately tarnish your image, lower your credibility, and give readers a good reason to delete your emails without reading any further.

There are many software tools that will help you gather and manage opt-in email lists and format professional enewsletters, blog posts, and marketing emails. Some of these tools include:

► Constant Contact: https://www.constantcontact.com/
► GetResponse: https://www.getresponse.com/
► Mailchimp: https://mailchimp.com/
► MailUp: https://www.mailup.com/

Out of all the promotional and marketing tools that allow you to reach out to your target audience, direct email is the most personal and can be highly effective if used correctly. Start building your email databases and encouraging everyone you encounter in the real world and online to opt into your email list.

Paid Advertising

In conjunction with all the free promotional opportunities you take advantage of (which still require your time to manage), one of the fastest ways to find potential new clients is to use paid, highly targeted advertising, both online and in the real world.

▶ Be Careful Whom You Trust

If you go to ad sales representatives from Google or Facebook for help with your ad campaign, they won't necessarily understand what your business is all about or which target audience you're trying to reach. They just want you to believe that their platform is the very best place for you to spend your ad dollars. Their goal is to sell you as much online advertising as possible.

If you're new to online advertising, consider hiring a virtual assistant with experience in this field to help you design and manage your campaigns and leverage your spending as much as possible to achieve your objectives. This approach can save you a lot of time, money, and possibly aggravation.

Whether you work with an online advertising expert or decide to create and manage your own campaigns, pay careful attention to the real-time analytics provided by the platform as your ads run. This will help you fine-tune your campaigns, determine what's working, and reallocate money when your ads are not achieving the desired results.

Social media advertising (on Facebook, Instagram, LinkedIn, or Twitter, for example) and search engine advertising (via Google Ads, for example) cost money, but they can help you quickly reach potential clients that fit your target demographic. Keep in mind that every online advertising opportunity works a bit differently, so before investing a lot of money in a campaign, make sure you fully understand how advertising on that platform works, and that you're using the ad(s) that will appeal most to your selected audience.

In addition to social media and search engine advertising, another option is to advertise on well-established podcasts or blogs that reach your target audience.

How quickly you're able to find and land new clients using paid online advertising will depend on how well you design the campaign, how effectively you're able to reach your target audience, and how much money you can spend.

Keep in mind that for advertising to work, someone typically needs to see your ad multiple times before they'll respond to it. Achieving multiple ad impressions costs money, so make sure you have the budget to keep your ad campaign going long enough to have the desired impact.

Beyond the advertising opportunities available online, there are many types of advertising opportunities in the real world. However, you should concentrate your ad spending on highly targeted advertising that reaches your potential clients. Thus, consider advertising with special-interest or topic-specific publications and media outlets, for example.

If you advertise in a general-interest publication, or on a radio or TV show or in movie theaters, only a small portion of the audience will likely be interested in hiring a virtual assistant. The same is true if you advertise in mass-market, consumer-oriented newspapers or magazines. These advertising options work best if your company truly caters to a broad, mass-market audience, as opposed to a niche audience.

Again, determine the media consumption habits of your potential clients and try to reach them with ads in media outlets you know they read, listen to, or watch regularly.

Tap the Power of the Media with a PR Campaign

Another piece of your overall marketing efforts can include public relations. Your goal is to compile a targeted list of editors, journalists, show hosts, podcasters, bloggers, and producers who work for media outlets that reach your target audience (i.e., potential clients). By providing them with press releases and other information, you want to entice them to include information about your company and its services in their editorial coverage.

Beyond just getting your virtual assistant business mentioned in an article, you could also try to get yourself interviewed as an expert in your field by reaching out to newspapers, magazines, radio shows, TV shows, news-oriented websites, online publications, blogs, podcasts, and other media outlets.

Keep in mind that some blogs and podcasts have larger readerships and more dedicated audiences than mainstream newspapers and magazines. In addition, there are blogs and podcasts for just about every topic imaginable and every possible target audience— including small business owners, entrepreneurs, and others who would benefit from hiring a virtual assistant.

If you're not familiar with how public relations works, seriously consider hiring a freelance PR specialist (or a virtual assistant with PR experience), who will already have established media contacts and can help you reach your target audience. A more costly option is to hire a PR firm to create and manage your entire campaign, but this will cost between $2,000 and $10,000 per month. To generate the best results, a PR campaign should run for at least three to six months.

Just about everything you'd hire a freelance PR specialist or PR firm to handle on your behalf can be done yourself. But it takes time to learn the right skills, develop your media list, and reach out in the correct way.

At the core of every PR campaign is one or more well-written press releases. A press release is typically a one-page, news-related announcement that adheres to a very specific format. It provides journalists with the core facts they need to (in theory) write an article.

A press release needs to be targeted to the media outlet it's being sent to, well-written, informative, and convey the basic information (i.e., who, what, where, when, why, and how) in the most attention-getting but concise way possible.

At the top is a catchy and to-the-point headline. Immediately below that is contact information for the person, company, or organization sending out the press release, followed by a few short paragraphs containing the core message. If a press release is done correctly, a journalist will have everything they need for their media coverage, or at least contact the person who sent the release to schedule an interview or request more information.

It's essential that you format the press release correctly and send it to appropriate members of the media. You can find more information about how to write and format a press release at PRWeb (https://service.prweb.com/resources/release-ideas) or CBSNews.com (https://www.cbsnews.com/news/how-to-write-a-press-release-with-examples/).

Beyond press releases, a PR campaign might include creating and distributing more elaborate press kits to select media outlets. A press kit includes press releases, a company "backgrounder" (detailed background information, such as a history of the company or financial statistics), biographies of the company's leaders, clips from recent media coverage, and other pertinent information. It might also include photos of company executives and/or products, along with the company's logo.

In addition to creating well-written and attention-getting press releases and PR materials, another part of an effective public relations campaign is compiling a targeted media list and then contacting the appropriate journalists, editors, reporters, show hosts, producers, podcasters, and/or bloggers. To help with this aspect of a PR campaign, you can purchase media directories and customized lists of media outlets, as well as lists of media professionals who cover specific topics.

Some companies sell media directories or lists of media professionals include Cision (www.cision.com/products/database/) and Easy Media List (www.easymedialist.com/).

There are also press release distribution services that will distribute your pre-written press release(s) to specific types of media outlets for a fee. Some of these services include:

- ▶ Business Wire: https://www.businesswire.com/portal/site/home/
- ▶ EIN Presswire: https://www.einpresswire.com/
- ▶ eReleases: https://www.ereleases.com/
- ▶ Newswire: https://www.newswire.com/
- ▶ PR Newswire: https://www.prnewswire.com/
- ▶ PRWeb: https://www.prweb.com/
- ▶ Send2Press: https://www.send2press.com/

Meanwhile, if you're looking to get booked on talk radio shows to promote your VA business, you can contact program producers at radio stations that cater to your target audience, or you can run a paid ad in the *Radio-TV Interview Report* (https://www.rtir.com/), which is a monthly publication that gets mailed to thousands of talk radio show producers and serves as a sourcebook for talk show guest ideas and recommendations.

There are also free and low-cost databases and services that will help you get booked as a guest on popular podcasts. If this is of interest to you, check out what's offered by Guest.Market (https://guest.market), MatchMaker.fm (https://www.matchmaker.fm/), and PodcastGuests (https://podcastguests.com/directory).

Running a PR campaign allows you to receive free media coverage and potentially boost awareness of your company. The drawback is that you don't control when the media coverage will run or the exact message that's published. The journalist is free to write or say whatever they want about your business.

However, if you carefully craft your press releases and press kit, provide quality images (when applicable), and approach media professionals with a similar target audience, you'll find that they will often rely heavily on your materials when creating their coverage. Your core message might even be reproduced word-for-word—or at least the main concepts behind your core message will be conveyed.

When dealing with the media, it's important to understand that every media outlet runs on a lead time and has nonnegotiable deadlines. Become familiar with the schedule of your targeted media outlets before you make contact, and then plan your PR campaign accordingly.

Also realize that journalists working under tight deadlines have a job to do and are constantly being approached by people, companies, and organizations seeking free publicity just like you. Remember to be considerate and avoid harassing them.

"Experts Say . . ."

If you are an expert on a specific topic, you can use traditional PR methods to make yourself available as a guest or interview subject for related news, business, or human-interest stories.

The best way to reach out to media outlets is to create and distribute a press release, or to create a full digital press kit related to your business that you send to guest bookers, reporters, producers, podcasters, bloggers, YouTube channel hosts, and journalists who cover a specific subject matter. You can send your printed press kit via U.S. mail, but these days, most companies rely on email. Use your press materials to introduce yourself to journalists, editors, etc., and try to develop a long-term relationship with them, so anytime they need an "expert" in your field, you become the person they call on.

Once you've written one or more press releases, be sure to make them available on your company's website (in a "For the Media" or "Press" section). This section of your website should also include a detailed description of the business, biographies of your company's leaders, and other resources relating to your company and its specialties that someone in the media might find useful. In other words, make your digital press kit (which is an electronic and downloadable version of your regular press kit) easily accessible from your website.

tip

As opposed to working with national media outlets, it's always easier to obtain free publicity or get yourself interviewed or booked as a guest on niche-oriented blogs or podcasts and on YouTube channels, so this is a good place to begin.

In-Person and Online Networking

If you are in the same geographic area as many of your potential clients, one of the best ways to promote yourself and your business is to participate in networking opportunities that attract them. This might mean attending:

- ► Business expos
- ► College and university alumni events
- ► Events hosted online and IRL by Facebook groups
- ► Happy hour networking meetups (for businesspeople, entrepreneurs, or people working in a specific field/industry)
- ► Industry-specific trade shows or conferences
- ► Local chamber of commerce meetings (a state-by-state directory can be found here: https://www.uschamber.com/co/chambers)
- ► Local chapter meetings of national trade associations
- ► Local Meetup (https://www.meetup.com/) events. This organization maintains a database listing thousands of local meetups and networking opportunities, each targeted to a specific audience.
- ► Rotary meetings (https://www.rotary.org/en)
- ► Women in Business events (https://womeninbusiness.club/)

When attending any type of professional networking opportunity (even a virtual one), dress professionally, be ready to start conversations with prospective clients, and have plenty of business cards and brochures ready to distribute. There are many services, like Switchit (www.switchitapp.com), Dot (www.dotcards.net/), and HiHello (www.hihello.me), that allow you to create digital business cards that can be emailed, sent via text message, or shared via social media. These are ideal for online-based networking events, for example.

If you're not sure how to initiate a professional conversation with a stranger, check out the ideas for icebreakers offered by the Career Contessa website (https://www.careercontessa.com/advice/icebreaker-questions).

Based on your areas of expertise and the type(s) of clients you're looking to attract, consider putting together an informative or instructional 45-minute presentation that you can offer for free at trade shows, networking events, or via videoconference that would introduce what you do to attendees. While you want to promote your business during the presentation, it should not be a sales pitch. Possible topics might be:

▶ "How a Virtual Assistant Can Save You Time Managing Your Schedule"
▶ "Ten Ways a Virtual Assistant Can Save Your Business Money"
▶ "Ten Ways Lawyers Use Virtual Assistants"
▶ "Ten Ways Business Consultants Can Use a Virtual Assistant to Enhance Their Productivity"

Once you identify trade shows you could present at, contact the management company that produces each show and offer your services. To research industry-specific trade shows (both in-person and virtual ones), check out the trade-show directories on these websites:

▶ 10Times: https://10times.com/tradeshows/by-industry
▶ Absolute Exhibits: https://absoluteexhibits.com/top-100-usa-shows
▶ EventsEye: https://www.eventseye.com/index.html
▶ Events in America: https://eventsinamerica.com/events/trade-shows/2021

The Small Business Expo (https://www.thesmallbusinessexpo.com/) produces a trade show that's held in 45 U.S. cities each year and that caters to small business owners, entrepreneurs, and startups. The producers regularly invite speakers to present lectures on a wide range of topics, many of which relate to services a virtual assistant might provide. Speaker applications should be submitted here: https://www.thesmallbusinessexpo.com/speaker-submission/.

Volunteer for Causes and Organizations You Care About

There are countless nonprofit groups and charities constantly seeking volunteers with specific skill sets. By volunteering for an organization or at an event, you have a chance to meet and interact with new people, showcase your skills in a real-world setting, and impress prospective clients who share an interest in the company, group, event, or organization you're volunteering for.

If you're a virtual assistant who specializes in working with lawyers or law practices, for example, consider volunteering at events sponsored by your state bar association. Virtually every industry has at least one professional association that hosts local, state, and national meetings or conferences.

Word-of-Mouth Promotion and Referrals

Perhaps the most powerful marketing tool at your disposal is word-of-mouth promotion from current and past clients, former co-workers from your previous jobs, friends, relatives, and other people who know you and will happily recommend you or refer you to people they know. A personal recommendation or referral typically holds a lot of weight and offers a way for you to quickly build credibility with potential clients.

Join Professional Associations

There are several professional associations specifically for virtual assistants that provide a wide range of services to their members, from networking opportunities to training. Keep in mind that it's common for VAs to recommend other VAs they know and respect to their own clients, especially when their client needs services they can't provide. By developing a vast network of fellow VAs, you can take advantage of these referrals as a powerful way to generate new business.

Some of the more prominent professional associations that cater specifically to virtual assistants include:

▶ Association of Virtual Assistants: https://associationofvas.com/
▶ Global Alliance of Virtual Assistants: https://globalava.org/
▶ International Association of Professional Virtual Assistants: https://www.iapcollege.com/program/membership-virtual-assistants/
▶ International Virtual Assistants Association: https://ivaa.org/
▶ National Association of Virtual Assistants: https://www.nationalassociationofvas.com/
▶ VAnetworking.com: https://www.vanetworking.com/

There's no need to join all these professional associations. Check out their websites and then choose which will provide you with the most valuable resources, based on the cost of their annual membership.

Beyond the professional associations for virtual assistants, if you specialize in working with clients in a specific industry, becoming active in that industry's association(s) can provide you with prequalified client leads and ways to interact with them.

Advice from Melissa Smith, Founder and CEO of the Association of Virtual Assistants

Melissa Smith is not only a successful virtual assistant, but she's also the founder of The PVA (https://thepva.com/), a firm that matches clients with the right virtual assistants.

In 2019, she also founded and now serves as the CEO of the Association of Virtual Assistants (https://associationofvas.com/), one of several professional organizations for VAs that offers a wide range of resources, including training and networking opportunities, to its members. There are three membership tiers, ranging from $35 per month (or $397 per year) to $200 per month (or $2,397 per year).

In this interview, Smith shares her advice for up-and-coming virtual assistants and explains why joining a professional association can be beneficial.

What's your professional background, and how did you initially become a virtual assistant?

Melissa Smith: My mother was an assistant, so I knew from an early age that was something I wanted to do. I went to secretary school. My original focus was on being a medical secretary. I did this job for a short time, but I never really liked it. I also figured out that I had no interest in working directly in the corporate world. I later found that my skills and interests were better suited to working in the education field, as an assistant within private schools and universities. Back then, I found myself changing jobs every two to three years, because I got bored, or I wanted a raise that I was not given.

In September 2012, my husband committed suicide when I was three days into a new job. At that time, everything turned upside down for me. After moving from Georgia to California with my daughter to pursue a different job, about a year later, my daughter, who was going into her senior year of high school, really wanted to move back to Georgia. When I told my boss this, he said he did not want to lose me. He then created a virtual position for me that allowed me to do most of the work I was previously doing, but I was able to work from home in Georgia. I became that company's first remote employee.

After a few months of working remotely for this one employer, I began to think to myself, how would it work if I started my own business as an independent virtual assistant? I decided to give it a try. It was in December 2014 that I quit my steady virtual job and launched my own VA business, called The PVA. Its focus was on providing executive virtual assistant services.

Ultimately, I discovered that offering executive virtual assistant services was not necessarily what clients wanted to pay me to do. My first few clients were business professionals who also wanted to write books and who wanted me to handle this process for them. Through networking, I began meeting a lot of potential clients who wanted to hire me for tasks I had no interest in performing. About a year into running the virtual assistant business, I changed my focus from serving as a VA myself to serving as a matchmaker between independent virtual assistants and companies looking to hire a virtual assistant. This turned out to be the service that people really wanted from me.

I now train VAs to successfully run their own virtual assistant business, but I do not teach them the skill set related to their own area of expertise or specialty. In 2017, I also began doing some remote work consulting for businesses, and I teach them how to hire and work with virtual employees.

When I first started doing this, I had zero competition. At the same time, people did not really understand what I was doing. I really focus on communication strategy when creating the perfect VA and client fit. I have a 98 percent successful match rate.

What qualities make up the ideal virtual assistant, in your experience?

Smith: The perfect virtual assistant will really understand their value and who values them. We all look in the mirror often, but that does not mean we're actually seeing the correct image in the mirror. People often have a view of themselves that is inaccurate. When a VA starts out in this profession, they don't know everything. There will be a lot for them to figure out along the way. My job is to analyze a VA's skill set and experience and help them pinpoint where their value is and identify the types of clients that would be apt to pay them the most for their specialized services.

The best virtual assistants also understand what they do not want to do and what they're not good at, and they do not accept clients that will demand that they handle these tasks or services. In my opinion, a virtual assistant should strive to position their company as a boutique virtual assistant business that offers highly premium services to a select few clients. The alternative is to be a Target-like agency that offers a lot of services to a vast array of clients, and that generates their money from quantity, not necessarily the quality of their work.

What would you say are the most important personality traits a virtual assistant should possess?

Smith: It's knowing your communication style and knowing what you like and dislike. Too often, VAs conform, and they become frustrated later. VAs need to know how they work best and what allows them to be productive, so that they set up their business in a way that matches their desired lifestyle. Will the services you offer as a VA allow you to live your desired lifestyle? A VA also needs to develop a clear understanding about the type of client that will appreciate them and their value.

How important is it for an up-and-coming VA to have a niche or specialized skill set?

Smith: The riches are in the niches. You can be a successful VA and not have a niche. If you want to identify as a jack-of-all-trades, that might be appealing to you, but that type of success takes longer, because potential clients do not know how to identify or utilize you. If someone asks you what you do, and you reply "Everything," that will really confuse potential clients.

Always consider the 80/20 theory, which means that 80 percent of our business comes from 20 percent of our services. This is the mathematical equation that makes niching so powerful. Everyone should have some diversity in their services list. Keep in mind, however, that niching is for now, not forever. Niching should not be confused with how you diversify your income as a virtual assistant. Especially in the beginning, I believe people need to understand what you do. Someone should be able to say "Go to Melissa if you want to hire the right virtual assistant to do XYZ. She's the best at XYZ you can get."

How important is building a brand around yourself and your business as a virtual assistant?

Smith: When you're first starting out as a VA, you really have no idea why people are hiring you, so having a narrowly focused brand may not be appropriate. First figure out where the money is coming in from, and then slowly build your brand around why people are actually hiring you. You need to really understand why people are hiring you over someone else before you can create a brand. My brand as a VA is a mindset. It has nothing to do with a logo or a special color scheme. My brand is all about clients who believe that they cannot do it all by themselves. Anyone who believes they can find and hire a VA on their own would not hire me. My clients have the philosophy that they don't have the time to get it right, and they can't afford to get it wrong. Any money you spend branding your business at the start will need to be spent again down the road once you're established.

What is the Association of Virtual Assistants, and why did you create it?

Smith: It's something that I wanted to do since I first became a virtual assistant. I wanted real-time resources and mentors who could help me right from the start. My goal was to create a large and interactive community for VAs, because I think being part of a community so you can learn, grow, and communicate is essential for success.

Starting a professional association was something I placed on my vision board for the future. I knew in the beginning that I was not ready to take on this endeavor, but I knew that someday I would be. I started the association simply by sending out an email to all the virtual assistants I had ever encountered over the years and asking, "Who wants to help change the virtual assistant world with me?" I quickly got favorable responses, and we started this association after coming up with a series of objectives related to the organization's goals. Today, the association offers a wide range of tools, training, and resources for people at all levels working in this field.

Why would someone first starting out as a VA want to join a professional association?

Smith: For the resources, support, and feedback we provide. The main issues for remote workers, including virtual assistants, are dealing with the isolation and loneliness that come with working alone from home. These are issues we help VAs successfully deal with by providing social opportunities that are always available via Slack, for example.

Just like every other industry, we believe that everyone should be well-connected to their industry and know everything that's happening within it. VAs should want to ask questions and have a desire to expand their education and skill set. For all these things, we offer resources. The association offers real-time support that people can access every day, or whenever it's needed. We are building a very diverse but like-minded community that welcomes all virtual assistants, regardless of their experience level or niche.

One of the resources we offer is assistance for a VA when it comes to setting their pricing in the United States and Canada. We have developed industry-standard pricing that VAs can use as a reliable guideline, based on their specialty and experience. We also developed a way for VAs to earn specific certifications based on courses they take through our partners.

What is some advice you can offer a VA about how to set their rates?

Smith: This is a mindset. Set your rates based on your value. Understand the short- and long-term value you can provide to clients, and then start basing your pricing on that. Figure out how much money you need to make, how many hours you can work per month, how much profit you want to earn, and then how many clients you need to take on. Use this information to help you crunch numbers and come up with a pricing model for yourself and your services.

I suggest always seeking prepayment from your clients. You may start billing hourly, but you may discover that charging a flat rate for certain projects will be more beneficial to your financial needs. When you charge by the project, you're charging for the value of your services, not the value of your time. There's a distinction here that you need to understand.

What are some of the biggest mistakes you see virtual assistants making?

Smith: The biggest mistake is when virtual assistants don't charge enough for their work, and they charge well below industry standards, because they don't understand their value. There are also VAs who give away too much of their time for free to be nice to their clients. You may be asked to do a task that is very easy for you, but that has a value to the client. However, because you perceive it as effortless, you undercharge or throw it in for free. That's a mistake.

Another mistake I see VAs make is not saying no to clients. First, don't take on clients you can't service. Once you've taken on a client, don't take on tasks that you really hate doing or that you're not qualified to do.

Do you have any advice on how a VA can better manage their time and avoid burnout?

Smith: Again, think about your time. How much time do you want to work in a week? Whatever time you initially allocate for client work, add another ten at the bare minimum. As a virtual assistant and business owner, you need to be your own client and take care of your own needs and the needs of your business. This is time you need to spend working, but that you don't bill out to other clients. Make sure you allocate the time needed to manage and operate your business, and then focus on the needs of your clients.

Keep in mind, you may discover it's beneficial to hire your own virtual assistant to help with the management of your business. You may discover that it makes sense for you to hire a nanny, or a cleaning person, to help you gain back time in your day. Don't take on too much at once, or you will eventually burn out. Take vacations and take breaks during your day. It is possible to implode your VA business by working too hard.

Work for an Agency

As you already know, the easiest way to work as a part-time or full-time virtual assistant without having to focus on finding and landing clients is to work for a well-established, reputable virtual assistant agency. You will earn less money, but working with an agency means you won't need to worry about all the aspects of running a business.

You'll have the best experience working for an agency if you choose one that will work to take full advantage of your skill set and work experience and match you with the most suitable clients. That way it can charge top dollar for your services.

Do your research before you commit to working for an agency. Make sure the business relationship appeals to you financially, based on the number of hours you'll be working, and get to know the culture of the agency beforehand to help ensure you'll get along well with the management and your fellow VAs.

Determine exactly what benefits the agency will offer to you as a subcontractor. A few questions you should ask include:

- ▶ Will there be opportunities for training and networking?
- ▶ What services does the agency provide to its VAs?
- ▶ Will you have any say over which tasks you're hired to perform for the clients or the specific clients you'll be working with?
- ▶ If you later decide to become an independent VA, will the agency try to enforce a noncompete clause in your contract?

Find VA Listings on Job Websites

Many online services post job listings from individuals and companies looking to hire a virtual assistant. In some cases, these clients are not looking for a long-term relationship, and only want help completing a specific task or project. Some of these services have no geographic limitations, so you will often be competing for VA jobs with people from other countries, who may be willing to work for much less money. Many of these services also charge a subscription fee to access job listings or take a percentage of the fees you're paid by the clients.

Most of these services rely on a rating and review system. As you're first getting started, you'll be competing with VAs who have already developed a favorable reputation on that service, so you could initially find yourself at a disadvantage.

However, finding and applying for VA jobs from one of these services offers a way to gain real-world experience as you get started. So later, when you seek out higher-paying clients on your own, you'll be able to demonstrate what you've done and how you've successfully used your skill set.

Some of the online services that publish job listings for virtual assistants include:

- ▶ Fiverr: https://www.fiverr.com/
- ▶ FlexJobs: https://www.flexjobs.com/
- ▶ Freelancer: https://www.freelancer.com/
- ▶ Indeed: https://www.indeed.com/
- ▶ People Per Hour: https://www.peopleperhour.com/
- ▶ Remote.co: https://remote.co/remote-jobs/
- ▶ TaskRabbit: https://www.taskrabbit.com/
- ▶ Time etc: https://web.timeetc.com/
- ▶ Upwork: https://www.upwork.com/
- ▶ Virtual Office Temps: https://www.virtualassistantjobs.com/

▶ WAHM.com: https://wahm.com/jobs.html

▶ We Work Remotely: https://weworkremotely.com

You've Found a New Client—Now What?

Finding clients who are interested in working with you is an important first step toward making your virtual assistant business successful. The next steps involve landing, onboarding, and then managing those clients with the goal of building long-term and mutually beneficial relationships. That's the focus of the next chapter.

Landing and Managing Your Clients

U p until now, you've been reading about the responsibilities of a virtual assistant, how to start your own VA business, and how to find potential clients. Once you get to the point where a client wants to hire you for short-term or long term work, this marks the beginning of a professional relationship, and that relationship should be treated with the utmost care.

All your interactions with a client need to be friendly and professional. Early on, you'll want to learn as much about your client as possible, define their needs, determine their objectives, pinpoint the challenges they're facing, and discover their work flow process. It's your responsibility to fit within that process so you can collaborate and communicate with each client as efficiently as possible.

As you'll discover, accomplishing this will require research, clear communication with your client, and the ability to listen and respond to what they have to say. Especially when you're first starting out, or anytime you begin working with a new client, unless you're specifically asked to come up with "a better way of doing things," you should handle the tasks and projects that are assigned to you by following the exact steps or directives provided by your client.

Once you know what the client is looking for, it's your job to help them figure out the best ways to use your time

warning

In most situations, wait until after you've proved yourself to your client and developed a relationship with them before you begin making suggestions about how they could improve their work flow. In most cases, if suggestions or feedback are wanted, the client will ask for them. Learn how to read the situation before you overstep and potentially tarnish your relationship with a client.

and skill set. Ultimately, it's on you to complete the work assigned to you in a correct and timely manner. Mistakes on your part can be frustrating and costly for your client and could jeopardize your relationship with them.

Do Your Research

Unless you're called out of the blue by a potential client, before you have that initial discussion about what you can do for them and how much your services cost, do as much preliminary research about them as possible.

A good place to start is their website. If the client has a LinkedIn account, this too will likely provide you with insightful information, as will reviewing their other social media accounts. Try to learn what the company does, how they do it, what sets them apart from their competition, what challenges the company and industry are facing, and what the company's culture is like.

The Client Interview Process

When you do have that initial phone conversation or virtual meeting with the client, ask insightful questions to make it clear you already know something about their company and industry. Then, based on your experience and skill set, focus on how you can address the client's wants and needs in a way that will prove beneficial and appealing to them. Again, listen carefully to what the client is telling you.

Especially once your business is more established, you'll want to use your research and initial conversations with the potential client to make sure they're a good fit for you, and you'll be a good fit for them. If your personalities clash, they require work you don't want to do or can't do, or if the client seems overly demanding, for example, you might want to refer them to another virtual assistant who might be a better fit.

Another thing you want to establish during those initial calls or meetings are realistic expectations regarding what you can do for the client, how quickly you'll be able to do it, and what the total costs will be. If they assign a task or project thinking it will take you five hours to complete, but it can't be done properly in less than ten hours (and at a higher cost), tell them immediately. Make sure you and the client are clear about deadlines, costs, and what processes or procedures you will use.

Before a client hires you, you'll likely exchange at least a few emails and participate in one or more phone calls or virtual meetings. This is your primary chance to get to know the client and determine what will be expected of you. Ask plenty of questions, allow the client to get to know you, discuss your work habits, find out what collaboration and communication tools the client already uses, and determine the types of tasks or projects they want you to work on. While you should maintain a cheerful, positive, and highly professional attitude, now is the time to determine what problems could arise and figure out how to eliminate these issues before they become a reality.

Again, make sure you're creating realistic expectations for the client in terms of what they can expect from you, the time you'll dedicate to each task or project, the process you'll use to complete each task, the deadline, and the cost. Ultimately, you'll want to summarize all this in writing and in the contract you'll have the client sign.

warning

One of the biggest problems for virtual assistants when it comes to working with their clients is miscommunication or lack of communication. Yes, your client is busy, and you don't want to waste their time. However, not gathering enough information, or misunderstanding what they're asking of you, could lead to serious problems and mistakes that will be time-consuming and costly to fix. If something the client says or does is confusing or unclear, ask for clarification immediately. Then confirm that you understand, and make sure you're both on the same page before moving forward.

The Onboarding Process

Every virtual assistant has their own process for onboarding a new client, so depending on the work you'll be doing for your clients, you'll likely want to develop your own system. For some VAs, the onboarding process starts by providing an initial questionnaire to the client. In addition to asking a few questions about what the company does and what its needs are, you could ask questions like:

▶ Have you ever worked with a virtual assistant before?

▶ What primary tasks or projects are you looking to have a virtual assistant complete?

▶ How many hours per week of the virtual assistant's time do you anticipate needing?

▶ What online collaboration and communication tools do you currently use?

▶ Would you prefer communicating with your virtual assistant by phone, via a virtual meeting, via instant messaging, or by email?

▶ What tasks or projects are currently your biggest time suckers or time wasters that you'd like a virtual assistant to step in and handle?

tip

If the initial conversations are going well and the client is ready to assign specific tasks or projects to you, now that you've done some research and know something about the client, consider bringing up additional ways you could work together. You might be able to provide value to the client in ways they never realized were possible. You can do this at the very beginning of the relationship or wait until you've successfully completed one or two initial tasks or projects for that client.

At the same time you're asking questions, consider providing the client with printed (or emailed) information about your company, a short bio describing your skills and experience, your list of services, and details about your boundaries (see below). These documents will help your clients understand exactly what you can do and might inspire them to hire you for additional work.

Set Your Boundaries

Communication between you and the client needs to be consistent to develop clear expectations and a mutual agreement to work together in a productive manner.

You'll want to set and discuss your boundaries at the outset. For example, if your workday is between 9 A.M. and 5 P.M. in your time zone, you need to make it clear that unless there's an emergency, you're not available to the client before or after those hours on your scheduled workdays. You also need to spell out what access, if any, a client will have to you on weekends and holidays.

Another boundary might be deadlines. Unless a client has already booked your entire day or week, for example, they should not be allowed to call you with a last-minute task or project and expect it to be completed later that day. Spell out what your required lead time is and what hours or days you will be able to dedicate to that client. Make it clear that you can't be expected to drop whatever you're doing for another client on a frequent basis, and that new task requests will be handled within 48 hours, for example.

Boundaries can also relate to how and when you'll communicate with your client. For example, you can state that you're available once per week for a 30- or 60-minute phone call or virtual meeting, and then all other communication will be via email or instant messaging during your business hours. Depending on the relationship you're building with each client and what you'll be doing for them, these terms and boundaries will vary greatly. They should, however, be put into place right away to protect your interests while creating proper expectations for each client.

Over time, as you work with clients, you'll likely need to modify your boundaries. But whatever they are, they should be discussed in advance, put in writing, and included in your contract.

Spell It All Out in the Contract

Regardless of the work you'll be doing for a client, it is essential to have a written contract that's signed and dated by both parties before you begin working. This contract needs to be provided by you, the virtual assistant. There are two approaches to take. The first and most expensive option is to hire a lawyer to compose the contract for you from scratch. You can then modify it yourself for each client as needed.

The second, less expensive approach involves obtaining a contract template, customizing it yourself, and then having a lawyer simply review it. Free contract templates are available online, and some of the professional associations for virtual assistants provide them to members. Search online for "virtual assistant employment contract" or "virtual assistant employment contract template" to see what's available.

For example, the HoneyBook software for virtual assistants offers a module with sample employment contract templates that you can modify and personalize within the application (https://www.honeybook.com/online-contract). You can then submit the final contract to clients and have them sign and return it digitally. DocuSign (https://www.docusign.com/) is one service you can use to automate this process.

The Bonsai website offers a free virtual assistant employment contract template and contract generator that you can use to create a personalized contract for you and your clients to sign (https://www.hellobonsai.com/a/virtual-assistant-contract). Anytime you come across a sample contract, always be sure to customize it to meet your needs and then have your own lawyer review it. You'll also find sample templates online by visiting:

- ▶ Indy: https://weareindy.com/blog/a-guide-to-virtual-assistant-contracts-and-templates
- ▶ The Pinnergrammer:
  https://thepinnergrammer.com/portfolio/free-virtual-assistant-contract-template
- ▶ Virtual Staff Finder: https://www.virtualstafffinder.com/virtual-assistant-contract-form/

According to the Bonsai website, "The contract is necessary to clarify the measures to take in case of a dispute between the client and his virtual assistant. The virtual assistant contract doesn't only focus on the clarifying issues around what the VA is supposed to do. It also delves into the payment terms." Keep in mind, your contract should also outline payment details and termination terms.

As for ending a working relationship with a client, there are several ways this can go. Either the VA can decide to terminate the deal, or the client can choose to fire the VA. The terms of the VA relationship termination should be included in your contract.

Depending on the work you'll be doing for your client, the contract you create could be formatted as a contractor agreement or retainer agreement. This describes the relationship between the virtual assistant and the client. In addition to focusing on the details of your business relationship, it should contain wording relating to confidentiality and nondisclosure.

In a nutshell, the contract you create should include seven core elements:

1. *Payment/retainer terms.* Describe when, how, and how much you'll be paid.
2. *Termination provisions and dispute resolution.* Specify how either the VA or the client can sever the relationship and on what grounds, and how disputes will be handled.
3. *Confidentiality.* State that proprietary information will be kept private.
4. *Restrictive covenants.* This might include a noncompete clause.
5. *Deliverables.* This section contains a description of exactly what's expected of the VA (the services to be provided), including deadlines, and how the work will be delivered (if applicable).
6. *Renewals.* Depending on the duration of the contract, include a clause about whether the contract automatically renews, or what the renewal procedure is.

7. *Boundaries*. Based on the type of work the VA will be doing, this could outline business hours, acceptable methods of communication, and a statement about how the VA will be treated by the client.

Sample Employment Contracts Between VAs and Clients

Chapter 9 includes a collection of in-depth interviews with successful and well-established virtual assistants who share their experiences, advice, and tips for people trying to establish themselves in this field.

Several of these VAs have graciously provided copies of their own VA employment contracts, so you can see firsthand what's included in them. Personal information, including their rates, has been removed. Refer to Figure 7–1 on page 127, Figure 7–2 on page 133, Figure 7–3 on page 142, and Figure 7–4 on page 146 for sample employment contracts.

Develop and Showcase Your Client Relations Skills

Over the course of your career, you've probably developed an extensive and marketable skill set. It's this skill set, along with your education, that will help you pinpoint your niche as a virtual assistant. However, if your skill set does not already include customer relations, you'll want to develop these skills before you start working with clients.

With proper research and screening before and during the client onboarding process, hopefully you can identify most of the potentially difficult clients and avoid working with them, or at least set mutually agreed-upon ground rules that make the experience manageable. After all, you're an independent contractor, not an employee.

But as you take on more and more new clients, you'll eventually experience disagreements and/or miscommunications with clients or encounter people who are overly demanding, obnoxious, rude, condescending, self-centered, narcissistic, or whom you just don't like. This is when your customer service skills really need to kick in. Even if you ultimately choose to fire the client, you don't want to burn any bridges or part ways on a sour note.

Client relations is all about acting professionally, problem solving, being polite, staying honest, showing empathy, and listening. You may also need confidence to stand up to a difficult client in a tactful way. Ideally you'll find a way to adapt and make the client happy without compromising your own integrity.

There are many resources, including books and online courses, to help you learn customer service skills. Some good options include:

- ▶ Dale Carnegie: https://www.dalecarnegie.com/en/topics/customer-service
- ▶ Disney Institute:
  https://www.disneyinstitute.com/disneys-approach-quality-service-online/
- ▶ HubSpot: https://blog.hubspot.com/service/customer-service-skills
- ▶ Lessonly: https://www.lessonly.com/customer-service-skills/
- ▶ ServiceSkills eLearning: https://go.serviceskills.com
- ▶ Udemy: https://www.udemy.com/topic/customer-service/

Not only will providing top-notch customer service to your clients increase renewals of existing contracts, but it'll also help increase word-of-mouth referrals and allow you to build a stellar reputation.

Advice from Business Leaders Who Rely on VAs for Their Success

Elsewhere in this book, you'll read interviews with highly experienced and successful virtual assistants and people working in this field. Let's take a few minutes, however, to learn from experts with a different point of view—employers who regularly hire and use virtual assistants to help their respective businesses succeed.

Meet John Gotschall, CEO of Coaching Financial Concepts

For almost 30 years, John Gotschall has been using the tools of insurance and investment to help businesses grow. His firm, Coaching Financial Concepts, offers a one-stop shop for small businesses that need to deal with insurance and other issues. About ten years ago, he began working with his first virtual assistant, Sue Harrawood, owner of Peace of Mind Virtual Assistance.

The two met at a local Business Advocates Council meeting in Springfield, Illinois, introduced by a friend of his who was already a client at Peace of Mind. At the time, Gotschall was taking on additional responsibilities, which included serving on the board of directors for a different company and for a nonprofit organization called Kids Above All. Harrawood also volunteered for this organization, and the board members saw firsthand how skilled and effective she was at her job.

Gotschall's schedule had become extremely busy, and he soon realized that he needed help managing his calendar. Having worked with Harrawood at Kids Above All, he decided she would make the ideal virtual assistant to help him with Coaching Financial Concepts.

What did you initially hire Sue to do for you?

John Gotschall: From Day One working with her, I put her in charge of managing my calendar and scheduling. Over the past decade, her responsibilities have morphed into a variety of additional tasks. For example, she handles my company's social media marketing, scheduling speaking engagements, and managing my Zoom meetings. She's become like an executive assistant, but she works virtually.

What would you say is the key to developing a long-term relationship with a virtual assistant?

Gotschall: You need to build trust with the virtual assistant you're working with. It's essential that you also develop a strong and open line of communication. The strengths of the client should also be the opposite of what the VA can do, so that together, you can handle everything necessary to run a successful business. For example, my strengths are presenting and sales, and Sue's is organization. We are a perfect fit. You also need to be able to give your virtual assistant direction, and then let them do what they do best.

As someone who relies on a virtual assistant, what personality traits do you think a VA should possess to be successful?

Gotschall: First and foremost, a virtual assistant should have great communication skills, especially because part of her work for me involves reaching out and interacting with my clients. I believe a virtual assistant should also have a high level of class and elegance about them, as well as a detail-oriented mindset. Organization and time management skills are important and key traits that I'd look for in a virtual assistant.

When I began working with Sue, what made her appealing to me was that I already had confidence in her and her abilities because I had seen her work firsthand through our volunteer work with Kids Above All. She had already demonstrated a consistent quality of work and excellent follow-through regarding everything she did. She carries herself in a very professional way and conveys herself as being a very honest and hardworking person.

Do you believe virtual assistants should offer highly specialized or niche-oriented services to their clients?

Gotschall: A virtual assistant should market what they do best, especially around those areas where business leaders most frequently need help. Working with Sue saves me at least 20 hours per week by handling my schedule and managing all aspects of my calendar. I am able to manage and grow my business more effectively because she frees up my time from having to do distracting or time-consuming tasks that don't rely on my own area of expertise.

Throughout your workday, how do you typically communicate with your virtual assistant?

Gotschall: We set up a weekly, one-hour meeting on the phone. Then, throughout the week, we keep in touch via telephone, text, and email. Since Sue knows where I am and what I am doing every minute of the day, she knows the best time and communication method to use. Our weekly phone meeting has proven very useful for staying on the same page, strategizing, and getting questions answered.

It sounds like for you, the biggest benefit has been improved time management. What would you say are the other good and bad things about working with a virtual assistant?

Gotschall: When I am having a difficult day, Sue is able to pick my spirits up. Because she now understands my business so well, she's also become a trusted sounding board for new ideas. Sue is a great listener and understands my situation, so she's able to provide valuable emotional support. I view Sue as a peer, not an employee. There's a mutual respect between she and I.

Because a virtual assistant has multiple clients, have there been scheduling conflicts that did not permit your VA to perform tasks when you needed them?

Gotschall: This problem has been very minimal, because of our weekly planning meetings. It's up to me as the business owner to be able to share whatever problem I am having, as well as its urgency, and then ask the virtual assistant to step in on an emergency basis only when it's necessary. I have reasonable expectations about when Sue is available, and I respect her time and that she has other clients. Sue knows that if I were to ask for something on an emergency basis, I am really dealing with a legitimate emergency.

Is there any other advice that you'd offer virtual assistants first entering this field?

Gotschall: Really work on your communication, organization, problem solving, and time management skills. As someone who hires and works with VAs, I look for people who are personable, professional, enthusiastic, and honest. I want to work with a virtual assistant who really wants to help my business stay successful and grow.

Meet Brad Farris, CEO of Anchor Advisors

Brad Farris' coaching and advising company focuses on helping other creative-services companies grow past the $1 million barrier. He's been doing this for more than 20 years.

What originally made you decide to hire virtual assistants?

Brad Farris: It was about five years into running my business that I began working with a business coach. She made me do a time study on myself. I had to write down how I spent every minute of my workday for a full week. When I did that, what slapped me in the face was that I was spending 20 percent of my time scheduling and rescheduling client meetings and managing my calendar. This was taking up almost one full business day per week.

I decided that if I could hire someone to do this for me, I'd be getting the equivalent of a full business day back every week in my schedule. This is what made me want to hire a virtual assistant to do nothing but manage my schedule and coordinate my meetings. These days, my virtual assistant also handles a variety of other tasks for me and my business.

What do you look for when hiring a virtual assistant?

Farris: Because my VA needs to interface directly with my clients and business prospects, I need someone who has a personality, demeanor, and executive presence that will impress the clients and maintain my company's reputation. I need someone who is detail-oriented and able to set priorities. I also look for someone who has experience doing the tasks I need them to do, so I use their past performance to predict their future performance working with me.

I don't tend to look for certifications unless that's a requirement for the work. For example, I have a VA who handles my company's bookkeeping, so I found someone who was QuickBooks certified. I have another VA who maintains my website. For them, I just looked at their past work and skill set.

How do you define the role of a virtual assistant?

Farris: The way I do it is that I write a detailed job description in advance, just like I would for a regular employee, and then I recruit based on the skill set, education, and experience that the position requires. Right now, I work with five different VAs, each with a different skill set. I assign tasks and projects based on what each can do best. Several of the VAs I now work with came as direct referrals from VAs I was already working with.

What do you think is the key for building a long-term relationship between a virtual assistant and their client?

Farris: Because the virtual assistant who manages my calendar and schedule knows where I am and what I am doing throughout the day, she knows the best times to reach me to check in. I find these quick check-in calls to be very helpful, and they've allowed me to really build trust with her. Working with someone who is proactive is something I really appreciate. I primarily use Slack to communicate with my VAs throughout the week; however, I always schedule at least one phone or video call with each of them on a weekly basis.

When I am working with a VA, I am always as explicit as I can be when I want something done in a certain way. However, when I know I need something done, but I don't know the most efficient or cost-effective way to do it, I want to rely on the virtual assistant to research and then implement the best approach to handle that task or project. I really value when a VA comes back to me and asks for clarification about something or specifically tells me that my instructions are inadequate or confusing.

What are your expectations for a virtual assistant related to how quickly they can handle the tasks or projects you assign?

Farris: When I am hiring a virtual assistant, I tell them what type of response time I generally need. For the VA who is handling my schedule, I often need them to respond to a request in less than one day. However, when I am working with the VA who handles my company's website, those requests typically don't need to be handled in less than a week. If I ever have an emergency or a request that's outside the norm, I will ask for a faster response time.

Meet Meredith Noble, Cofounder and CEO of SenecaWorks LLC

Based in Anchorage, Alaska, Meredith Noble's business SenecaWorks LLC (https://www.learngrantwriting.org/) teaches people who are looking for a career change how to become successful freelance grant writers, mainly for nonprofit organizations.

Noble is personally responsible for securing more than $45 million in grant funding for the nonprofit organizations she's worked with. She's also the author of *How to Write a Grant: Become a Grant Writing Unicorn,* a book published by her company and available from Amazon.

As a result of her business' steady, fast growth, Noble decided it would be to her advantage to hire a virtual assistant.

How did you go about hiring your first virtual assistant, and how was that experience?

Meredith Noble: The first VA I hired was not trained as a VA. She did not know how to handle core tasks, like inbox management or receipt management. I didn't realize right away that the experience was not working out well, but I did notice that my inbox, for example, never did get properly managed. Several months later, we parted ways, and I sought out a different virtual assistant.

For the second VA, I took a different approach to my hiring process. Instead of asking for a written application, I asked applicants to submit a short video of themselves describing why they wanted the job and were qualified to fill it. I was amazed at the diversity in the quality of the videos I received.

These application videos helped me decide if I was connected to that person and if it would ultimately be a good working relationship. Once I selected a handful of applicants who submitted videos that caught my attention, we further vetted them using more traditional methods. Currently, we have two virtual assistants that regularly work with us. One is a dedicated VA for me, and the other is a website designer who focuses just on our online presence.

How do you define the role of a virtual assistant?

Noble: A virtual assistant is someone who allows our company to move forward exponentially faster because they're removing the tasks that slow our in-house team down. The virtual assistant's role is a support role that allows us to spend time on other things.

What I love about working with a virtual assistant is that they take the tasks I hate most off my plate altogether. As a result, my happiness and productivity have gone way up.

Why did you want to hire a virtual assistant, as opposed to a full-time or part-time employee?

Noble: Ultimately, we wound up working with Latrice Prater from The Digital Solutions Team. Being in Alaska, I didn't care where our virtual assistant would be located, as long as the time difference was not too great. We wanted someone who was in a time zone that was no more than two or three hours different from ours. If I can communicate with our virtual assistant during our business day, I don't really care when they work or where they work from.

While Latrice has her defined business hours that we agreed to in advance, she is often willing to work other hours if the need arises. She does have a line in the sand, however, that she is never available on Saturdays, and we respect that

What communications tools do you use to stay in touch with your virtual assistant?

Noble: Slack is the primary tool that makes it possible for us to work with a virtual assistant. Except for a weekly, 30-minute video call that's held every Monday, all our communications and collaborations happen over Slack. We also use Asana for project management and planning.

What do you believe are the most important personality traits that a virtual assistant should possess?

Noble: Communication skills are essential. Another trait is their willingness to push back. If one of our VAs sees a better way of handling something or can recommend a better approach, I want them to speak up and share their ideas. It's these leadership skills that can help our company grow. I need our VAs to have initiative and their own critical thinking skills.

How did you determine your monthly budget for a virtual assistant?

Noble: Luckily, Latrice came to us with her price list, which included her hourly rate and a series of packages that each include a fixed number of hours per month. If we don't use all those hours, they don't roll over. We receive weekly reports that account for how much time we've used thus far.

I like this approach, because once we chose a package, I knew how much time per month the VA would be available to me, and I was easily able to budget for it as a fixed expense. For me, this works better than paying a VA by the hour without a package, because the monthly bill fluctuated wildly, which made our budget much harder to plan. I have no trouble paying our virtual assistants well, as long as they are highly efficient.

In your opinion, what's the best way to develop a positive, long-term relationship between a client and a virtual assistant?

Noble: The relationship between a virtual assistant and their client needs to go both ways. For us as a client, it has a lot to do with demonstrating appreciation in ways that are special. When someone feels appreciated, they do their best work. When our virtual assistant recently completed a major project for us, we thanked her using an ice cream delivery service and had three pints of gourmet ice cream delivered to her home for her family to enjoy.

Learn How to Manage Your Time

Once you've built up a full roster of clients, you'll need to perform the work of a virtual assistant, handle the tasks and projects that are assigned to you, manage your business, and juggle your other personal and professional responsibilities. The trick to success when it comes to multitasking a wide range of responsibilities on an ongoing basis is to develop superior organization and project management skills, as well as become an expert at time management. This is the focus of the next chapter.

Agreement for Services

This Agreement for Services ("Agreement") is entered into as of the ___ day of _____ 20__, between _____ ("the Contractor") and _____ ("the Company").

1. *Independent Contractor.* Subject to the terms and conditions of this Agreement, the Company hereby engages the Contractor as an independent contractor to perform the services set forth herein, and the Contractor hereby accepts such engagement.

2. *Scope of Work, Term, and Rate.* The Company hereby retains Contractor to provide the services detailed in Scope of Work for a minimum number of monthly hours, as detailed in the attached Exhibit A. The Contractor's Scope of Work, Term of Engagement, Rate, and the terms for Payment thereof shall be as set forth in the attached Exhibit A.

3. *Expenses.* During the term of this Agreement, the Contractor shall bill and the Company shall reimburse the Contractor for all approved out-of-pocket expenses. If travel expenses other than local travel are required, the Company shall reimburse the Contractor for the reasonable costs of travel incurred pursuant to the maximum per day rates as established by Public Law 99-234.

4. *Confidentiality.* Contractor has received, will receive, or will contribute to information not generally known and proprietary to Company about the business, customers, services, and products of Company ("Confidential Information"). Confidential Information includes, but is not limited to, customer and contact names, phone numbers, addresses, email addresses, order history, order preferences, chain of command, pricing information, and other information identifying facts and circumstances specific to customers and relevant to the Company's sales and services. All such information, together with all information relating to the terms and conditions set forth in this Agreement and the terms and conditions of Contractor's relationship with Company, is collectively referred to in this Agreement as "Confidential Information."

Contractor hereby acknowledges and agrees that all Confidential Information, including that concerning the business or affairs of Company, the Company's clients, and the terms and conditions of Contractor's relationship with Company, shall be maintained in strict confidence by Contractor and shall be used only for

FIGURE 7-1: **Sample Freelance Employment Contract #1**

the purpose of performing Contractor's Services pursuant to this Agreement, and that no such Confidential Information shall be otherwise used or disclosed by Contractor without the prior written consent of Company.

Upon termination of Contractor's relationship with Company, all Confidential Information and all other documents, records, notebooks, customer lists, business proposals, contracts, agreements, and other repositories containing information concerning Company or the business of Company (including all copies thereof) in Contractor's possession, whether prepared by Contractor or others, shall remain with, be destroyed, or be returned to Company. Contractor shall notify the Company immediately in the event Contractor becomes aware of any loss or disclosure of any Confidential Information.

Nothing herein shall be construed to prevent disclosure of Confidential Information as may be required by applicable law or regulation, or pursuant to the valid order of a court of competent jurisdiction or an authorized government agency, provided that the disclosure does not exceed the extent of disclosure required by such law, regulation, or order. Contractor agrees to provide written notice of any such order to an authorized officer of the Company within 48 hours of receiving such order, but in any event sufficiently in advance of making any disclosure to permit the Company to contest the order or seek confidentiality protections, as determined in the Company's sole discretion.

5. *Conflicts of Interest; Non-Hire Provision.* The Contractor represents that they are free to enter into this Agreement, and that this engagement does not violate the terms of any agreement between the Contractor and any third party. The Contractor is expressly free to perform services for other parties while performing services for the Company. During the period of this Agreement and for a period of twelve months following the termination of this Agreement, the Contractor shall not, directly or indirectly, hire, solicit, or encourage to leave the Company's employment any employee, consultant, or contractor of the Company or hire any such employee, consultant, or contractor who has left the Company's employment or contractual engagement within one year of such employment or engagement. During the period of this Agreement and for a period of twelve months following the termination of this Agreement, the Company shall not, directly or indirectly, hire, solicit, or encourage to leave

FIGURE 7–1: **Sample Freelance Employment Contract #1,** continued

the Contractor's employment any employee, consultant, or contractor of the Contractor or hire any such employee, consultant, or contractor who has left the Contractor's employment or contractual engagement within one year of such employment or engagement.

6. *Termination*. Either party may terminate this Agreement at any time by giving one month's written notice to the other party. In addition, if either party, or any of its owners, principals, officers, or directors is convicted of any crime that is a felony or involves fraud or dishonesty, the other party may immediately terminate the engagement and without prior written notice. In the event Company requests that Contractor act in a manner inconsistent with the law or if Contractor becomes aware of any illegal activity by Company, Contractor may immediately terminate the engagement and without prior written notice.

7. *Relationship of the Parties*. This Agreement shall not render the Contractor an employee, partner, or joint venturer of the Company for any purpose. The Contractor is and will remain an independent contractor in their relationship to the Company. The Company shall not be responsible for withholding taxes with respect to the Contractor's compensation hereunder. The Contractor shall have no claim against the Company hereunder or otherwise for vacation pay, sick leave, retirement benefits, Social Security, workers' compensation, health or disability benefits, unemployment insurance benefits, or employee benefits of any kind.

8. *Insurance*. The Contractor will carry liability insurance relative to any service that they perform for the Company.

9. *Indemnity*. To the fullest extent permitted by law, Company shall indemnify and hold harmless Contractor, its agents, employees, officers, directors, subcontractors, and insurers from any claim or action arising out of, alleged to arise out of, or related to Contractor's negligent acts or omissions while performing under this Agreement. Company's indemnity obligations shall not extend to reckless, malicious, or intentional acts or omissions.

10. *Choice of Law*. The laws of the state of _____, with the exception of its choice of law provisions, shall govern the validity of this Agreement, the construction of its terms, and the interpretation of the rights and duties of the parties hereto.

FIGURE 7–1: **Sample Freelance Employment Contract #1,** continued

11. *Maximum Liability for Damages.* Company agrees that Contractor's aggregate liability for any losses, damages, liabilities, judgments, interest, or awards of whatever kind, for breach of contract, tort, or any other cause of action arising under or related to this Agreement, shall in no event exceed the total of all amounts paid by Company to Contractor.

12. *Headings.* Section headings are for ease of reference, are not to be considered a part of this Agreement, and are not intended to be a full and accurate description of the contents hereof.

13. *Notices.* Any and all notices, demands, or other communications required or desired to be given hereunder by any party shall be in writing and shall be validly given or made to another party if personally delivered, or if deposited in the United States mail, certified or registered, postage prepaid, return receipt requested. If such notice or demand is served personally, notice shall be deemed constructively made at the time of such personal service. If such notice, demand, or other communication is given by mail, such notice shall be conclusively deemed given five days after deposit thereof in the United States mail addressed to the party to whom such notice, demand, or other communication is to be given as follows:

    If to the Contractor: _____

    _____

    If to the Company: _____

    _____

    Any party hereto may change its address for purposes of this paragraph by written notice given in the manner provided above.

14. *Modification or Amendment.* No amendment, change, or modification of this Agreement shall be valid unless in writing and signed by the parties hereto.

15. *Entire Understanding.* This document and any exhibit attached constitute the entire understanding and agreement of the parties, and any and all prior agreements, understandings, and representations are hereby terminated and canceled in their entirety and are of no further force and effect.

FIGURE 7–1: **Sample Freelance Employment Contract #1,** continued

16. *Unenforceability of Provisions.* If any provision of this Agreement, or any portion thereof, is held to be invalid and unenforceable, then the remainder of this Agreement shall nevertheless remain in full force and effect.

17. *Waiver.* Failure to invoke any right, condition, or covenant in this Agreement by either party shall not be deemed to imply or constitute a waiver of any rights, condition, or covenant and neither party may rely on such failure.

18. *Interpretation.* The parties hereby acknowledge that this Agreement represents the negotiated terms, covenants, and conditions of the parties, and the party responsible for drafting any such term, covenant, or condition shall not be prejudiced by any presumption, canon of construction, implication, or rule requiring construction or interpretation against the party drafting the same.

19. *Jurisdiction and Venue.* Each party irrevocably submits to the jurisdiction and venue of the state courts located in [county, state]_____ or the U.S. District Court for the District of [state]_____ in any legal suit, action, or proceeding arising out of or based upon this Agreement.

20. *Legal Representation.* The parties expressly acknowledge that they have been advised to seek independent legal counsel with respect to entering into this Agreement and have had adequate opportunity to do so.

IN WITNESS WHEREOF the undersigned have executed this Agreement as of the day and year first written above. The parties hereto agree that facsimile signatures shall be as effective as if originals.

Company: _____   Contractor:_____

Signed: _____   Signed: _____

Date: _____   Date: _____

FIGURE 7–1: **Sample Freelance Employment Contract #1,** continued

Exhibit A: Rate, Scope of Work, and Payment Terms

Start Date: _____

Term of Engagement: _____

Rate and Payment Terms (choose one):

$_____billed monthly for up to _____ hours per month. Unused hours are nonrefundable but roll over for 1 month. Additional hours as offered by the Company and accepted by the Contractor will be billed at $____/hour.

OR

$____ per hour, billed at the end of each month.

Special projects, such as website design, may be quoted separately.

Invoices are sent electronically the first business day of the month following work. Payment is due within 15 days of invoice. All invoices not timely paid in full will incur interest of 1.5 percent per month (18 percent per annum), or the maximum amount allowed by law, until paid in full.

Scope of Work:

Contractor's scope of work will primarily focus on: [Enter Scope]

_____

_____

_____

_____

The Company and Contractor recognize that the Scope of Work is fluid and may change based on the changing needs of the Company.

Company: _____   Contractor:_____

Signed: _____   Signed: _____

Date: _____   Date: _____

FIGURE 7–1: **Sample Freelance Employment Contract #1,** continued

Virtual Assistant Services Terms & Conditions Agreement

This agreement creates a contract made this ___ day of ___, 20___.

By and between: [VA Company Name] and [Client Company Name or Person]

WHEREAS, [Client Company Name or Person] shall be referred to as "Client," and [VA Company Name] shall be referred to as "VA."

WHEREAS, VA has a substantial background in administrative assistance and is willing to provide services to the Client based on this background.

WHEREAS, the Client desires to have services provided by VA.

NOW THEREFORE, it is agreed between the parties as follows:

1. *Description of Services.* VA will provide assistance to the Client as relative to the job description provided to VA by the Client, including but not limited to: [List Services Here]

   _____

   _____

   Any other services to be provided in the future shall be agreed upon by both parties in writing.

   This may exclude some specialty services (e.g., website creation/overhaul, grant writing, etc.).

2. *Subcontractors.* VA shall utilize the VA Virtual Assistants Subcontractor team as they deem necessary to complete Client tasks.

   If VA informs the Client that a project and/or service will be outsourced to a Subcontractor, the Subcontractor is the only employee other than VA who is permitted to complete the project or service. Additionally, the only information to be discussed between the Client and Subcontractor will be related to the assigned project or service.

   In no instance will the Client discuss with the Subcontractor financial information, including, but not limited to, payments that were made by and between the parties.

3. *Service Fees & Terms.* RETAINER

FIGURE 7–2: **Sample Freelance Employment Contract #2**

On the date of this Agreement, client has contracted VA for the following monthly retainer service(s) at the specified rate(s):

- Marketing Support: ____ hours per month at a rate of $____ per month.

- Administrative Support: ____ hours per month at a rate of $____ per month.

New Clients are subject to a one-time setup fee on the initial invoice.

If Client is eligible for an ongoing discount (i.e., Client has nonprofit status), Client's ongoing discount will begin after any initial promotions have concluded (if applicable).

Hours purchased for each service must be used solely for that service. Clients are unable to use hours from one service for another. Packages' hours will not roll over from one month to the next.

If VA is charged due to Client having insufficient funds for payment, the fees will be charged to Client. Rates are subject to increase up to 3 percent annually. Any rate changes will be provided to Client with 30 days' notice.

If Client surpasses monthly hours allotted, overage fees will apply and are based on the overage hours spent at the current agreed-upon package rate. If overage hours are not paid, overage hours will be subtracted from the following month's allotted hours.

Additional hours may be purchased mid-month at the current agreed-upon package rate.

Client Terms for packages and rates can be altered if there is written notice that is agreed upon by both parties.

*If no termination date is given, this agreement shall be effective until Client terminates the agreement by providing thirty (30) days of written notice to VA. Once notice is given, Client must pay through those 30 days and has 30 days to utilize current package.

A 30-day notice must also be given to reduce services by greater than 50 percent and to transition account to an hourly structure. If needed, there may be an option to pause services, which will require a payment of 25 percent of the current package rate(s) to be paid at the time of pausing. When services restart, that payment will be applied to the next invoice. If Client decides to terminate

FIGURE 7–2: **Sample Freelance Employment Contract #2,** continued

within the pausing period, that payment will be applied to Client's final 30-day notice invoice. VA may terminate services with Client at any time if the relationship is no longer a good fit, with or without cause, upon written notice.

Minimum hours for certain services may apply.

4. *Payment Policy.* Invoices will be sent on the first business day of each month through [Insert Service If Applicable] and are due on the invoice date.

Payment terms may change if agreed upon and signed by both the Client and VA.

Payments are to be made in U.S. Dollars, via credit card or ACH withdrawal.

In the event the Client does not pay invoice fees prior to the fifth day of the month, the credit card on file will be automatically charged on the fifth day of the month, including additional merchant processing fees when applicable. If the fifth falls on a weekend or holiday, payments will be processed the following business day.

If payment to VA is unable to be completed by charging the credit card on file, Client work will cease until remediation is made.

You authorize regularly scheduled charges to your checking, savings, or credit card account. You will be charged the amount for your monthly Service Packages, plus any additional charges based on hourly services and overage hours from the previous month and any applicable processing fees, each billing period. Aside from an invoice notification, you agree that no prior notification will be provided. If you need to make any changes to your payment method, you must notify VA before the fifth business day of the month.

I understand that this authorization will remain in effect until I cancel it in writing, and I agree to notify VA in writing of any changes in my account information or termination of this authorization at least 30 days prior to the next billing date. In the case of a transaction being rejected for Non-Sufficient Funds (NSF), I understand that VA may at its discretion attempt to process the charge again within 30 days, and I agree to an additional one-time $25 charge for NSF and inability to make payment. I acknowledge that the origination of these transactions to my account must comply with the provisions of U.S. law. I certify that I am an authorized user of this credit card account and will not

FIGURE 7–2: **Sample Freelance Employment Contract #2,** continued

dispute these scheduled transactions with my account holder, so long as the transactions correspond to the terms indicated in this form.

If you agree to the above statement, please initial here. _____

Please initial here if you would like us to automatically run your payments, including your initial payment and each month thereafter. _____ You will still receive invoice notifications, but you will not need to make payment on your end as we will complete payment on our schedule using your preferred payment method.

_____

Credit card information is required to complete this Agreement. VA will not begin work unless the information is provided.

Credit Card: A processing fee of 2.9 percent of the invoice price plus 30 cents is applied with this option:

❏ VISA   ❏ MasterCard   ❏ AMEX   ❏ Discover

Name on Card: _____

Credit Card #: _____

Exp: _____   CVV: _____

Billing Address: _____

_____

Phone Number: _____   Email: _____

*Client understands there shall be no refunds under any circumstances.

5. *Outstanding Invoices.* Late Payment Penalties as listed below will be incurred. In the event that the Client incurs an outstanding invoice, the charges shall accrue as follows:

10–16 days past due date: Client incurs a $95 late fee charge. VA reserves the right to refuse completion or delivery of work until past due balances are paid.

16–30 days past due date: VA reserves the right to refuse completion or delivery of work until past due balances are paid. Monthly late charges of $15 or 1.75 percent (APR of 21 percent), whichever is greater, will be assessed on unpaid balances every 30 days.

FIGURE 7–2: **Sample Freelance Employment Contract #2,** continued

30-plus days past due date: VA may use the services of a Collection Agency. Client will be responsible for any legal fees or filing fees if an unpaid invoice is sent to a Collection Agency.

If VA has submitted an invoice for the following month to the Client who refuses to make payment, the Client is in breach of this Agreement and the invoice will be sent to a Collection Agency.

6. *Referral Incentive.* If Client refers an individual to VA and that individual signs as a new client, Client will receive a one-time 10 percent discount on their next VA invoice after the new client is onboarded with VA.

7. *VA Office Hours.* VA and Team Subcontractors are generally available during office hours of [8 A.M.-5 P.M.] Mondays through Fridays in their given time zone.

VA and any Subcontractors will only service Client work outside office hours and on weekends at their own discretion. Should Client require weekend work or work outside office hours, Client will incur an additional $25 per hour rush fee that will be reflected on their invoice at the end of the month.

8. *Relationship of Parties.* It is understood by both parties that VA is an Independent Contractor and is not an Employee of the Client. The Client will not provide benefits, including health insurance, paid vacation, or any other Employee benefit for VA. VA is also responsible for his or her own taxes and other withholdings from his or her payments.

9. *Confidentiality.* The Client recognizes that VA may have the following proprietary information:

- Products
- Prices
- Costs
- Discounts
- Future plans
- Client database
- Business affairs
- Personal information
- Other information (collectively "Information") that is a valuable, special, and unique asset of the Client

FIGURE 7–2: **Sample Freelance Employment Contract #2,** continued

The Client's proprietary information will only be available to VA and Subcontractors working on Client's account. VA agrees not to, at any time or in any manner, either directly or indirectly, use any information for VA's own benefit, or divulge, disclose, or communicate in any manner any information to any third party without the prior written consent of the Client. VA will protect the Information and treat it as strictly confidential. A violation of this article shall be a material violation of this Agreement. The Client agrees to the same Confidentiality regarding the VA's proprietary information.

10. *Confidentiality After Termination.* The confidentiality provisions of this Agreement shall remain in full force and effect after the termination of this Agreement. The parties mutually agree to respect the information herein as confidential, provided that it is not public knowledge or available in public domain.

11. *Noncompetition.* Both Client and VA agree to noncompetition regarding their respective customers. Neither company will attempt to take any customers from the other company for any reason whatsoever. Any Client information will be kept confidential between the companies and will be used for the sole purpose of performing the contractual services as herein defined in this document.

    During the course of relationship with VA and for a period of 12 months after the cessation of the relationship for any reason, whether with or without cause, Client shall not directly or indirectly, either alone or in concert with others, solicit, entice, or in any way divert any of VA's Subcontractors, employees, or VA to do business with Client directly or any person in competition with VA, except as expressly permitted under this Section. Notwithstanding the foregoing restriction, at Client's election and with VA's and the respective employee or Subcontractor's approval, upon payment of [Insert Dollar Amount] to VA, Client may directly employ an employee or Subcontractor of VA as a virtual assistant, in which event this Agreement will immediately terminate. A lower payment may be agreed upon if Client retains additional services aside from the services provided by the employee or Subcontractor who will directly work with Client. In the case of a buyout agreement, it is understood that the Subcontractor is employed or contracted by Client directly at will, and the relationship between the employee or Subcontractor and the client is no longer monitored by VA.

12. *Source Files and Copyrights.* Client will retain all source files for all projects completed by VA, including their copyrights.

FIGURE 7–2: **Sample Freelance Employment Contract #2,** continued

13. *Client Representations*. Client represents and warrants that the text, graphics, and photographs provided to Designer for the Site are owned or licensed by Client, and that Client is authorized to use and display such items in the manner contemplated by this Agreement. Client shall be solely responsible for the Site and materials on the Site and the validity of copyrights, trademarks, and ownership claimed by Client. [Note: This paragraph deals with VAs working as a graphic artist or designer.]

Client agrees to indemnify and hold VA harmless from and against any claim, loss, damage, expense, or liability (including attorneys fees and costs) that may result, in whole or in part, from: i) any infringement or any claim of infringement of any trademark, copyright, trade secret, or negligence arising from any of the text, graphics, and photographs provided by Client; ii) any claim by a third party regarding any services or products sold or otherwise distributed by Client, its employees, or its agents; or iii) any claim, suit, penalty, tax, or tariff arising from Client's use of the internet or electronic commerce.

14. *Return of Records*. Upon termination of this Agreement, VA shall deliver all records, notes, data, memoranda, passwords, models, and equipment of any nature that are in VA's possession or under VA's control and that are the Client's property or relate to the Client's business.

15. *Entire Agreement*. This Agreement expresses the whole Agreement between the parties hereto as of the date hereof. This Agreement shall not be changed, modified, terminated, or discharged except by a writing signed by the parties hereto. This Agreement supersedes any prior written or oral agreement between the parties.

This Agreement may be modified or amended if the amendment is made in writing and is signed by both parties. Modifications or amendments to any Terms noted within this Agreement will be notified to Client via an online form that will have to be affirmed by the Client.

All notices required or permitted under the Agreement shall be in writing and shall be deemed delivered when delivered by facsimile, in person, or deposited in the United States mail, postage prepaid, or through secure website DocuSign to the intended party's current mailing address and email address, if applicable.

Both parties will alert the other of a change in contact information.

FIGURE 7–2: **Sample Freelance Employment Contract #2,** continued

16. *Severability.* If one or more of the provisions hereof shall be held to be invalid, illegal, or unenforceable, the validity and enforceability of its other provisions shall not be affected thereby.

17. *Waiver of Contractual Right.* The failure of either party to enforce any provision of this Agreement shall not be construed as a waiver or limitation of that party's right to subsequently enforce and compel strict compliance with every provision of this Agreement.

18. *Applicable Law.* This Agreement shall be governed by the laws of the State of [___], [USA], VA's state of business registration.

19. *Limited Liability.* VA's liability on any claim of any kind for any loss or damage arising out of, in connection with, or resulting from this agreement or from the performance or breach thereof shall in no case exceed the total amount of the invoice which gives rise to the claim.

20. *Marketing Materials and Contact.* I agree to allow VA to use any feedback of services provided, along with my name, company, and location, as testimonials on public mediums. _____ (please initial here)

    I am opting in to receiving phone text communication from the VA. _____ (please initial here)

21. *Please Read Items of Note.*

    1. Client understands there shall be no refunds under any circumstances.
    2. Hours purchased for each service must be used solely for that service. Clients are unable to use hours from one service for another.
    3. Package hours will not roll over from one month to the next.
    4. If no termination date is given, this agreement shall be effective until either party terminates the agreement by providing thirty (30) days of written notice to the other party. Once notice is given, Client must pay through those 30 days and has 30 days to utilize current package. A 30-day notice must also be given to reduce services by greater than 50 percent and to transition account to an hourly structure.
    5. Invoices will be sent on the first business day of each month and are due on the invoice date. In the event the Client does not pay invoice fees prior to the fifth day of the month, the payment on file will be automatically charged by VA on the fifth day of the month, including additional merchant processing

FIGURE 7–2: **Sample Freelance Employment Contract #2,** continued

fees when applicable. If the fifth falls on a weekend or holiday, payments will be processed the following business day.

22. *Signatures.* Please sign below if you agree to all the terms and conditions noted in this Agreement.

VA's Consultant Signature: _____

Consultant Name: _____ Date:_____

Client Signature: _____

Client Name: _____

Client Address: _____

_____

Client Phone: _____

Date: _____

FIGURE 7–2: **Sample Freelance Employment Contract #2,** continued

Contract Agreement for Virtual Assistant Services

Agreement made on _____, between BUSINESS NAME, a Sole Proprietorship organized and existing under the laws of the state of STATE, with its principal office located at BUSINESS ADDRESS, referred to herein as "Service Provider," and _____, with its principal office located at _____ _____, referred to herein as "Client."

For and in consideration of the mutual covenants contained in this agreement, and other good and valuable consideration, the receipt and sufficiency of which is acknowledged, the parties agree as follows:

Services. Client has hired Service Provider to perform virtual assistant services, which are: [Describe Services Here]

_____

_____

Payment: Client agrees to a monthly retainer of $_____ for services of _____ hours per month.

Monthly retainers are set to ensure ongoing support at a discounted rate up to the number of hours set forth in the agreement. Retainer fees are required in full in advance of services. Payment is due in full on the first of each month. If the payment is not received by the fifth, a late fee of $25 will be added to the monthly amount. Payments rendered are considered fully earned and nonrefundable. Unused hours are not carried over into the next month.

Client agrees to an hourly fee of $_____ per hour.

Time is tracked and billed to the nearest 15-minute increment. Client will be invoiced for hours billed monthly.

Client agrees to a project-based fee of $_____ for completion of the project detailed in the attached project proposal.

A 50 percent deposit is due upon project proposal acceptance. The remaining 50 percent is due upon completion and delivery of the project.

Additional Work: Client understands that additional work beyond the scope of this agreement must be negotiated separately and will require a separate agreement.

FIGURE 7–3: **Sample Freelance Employment Contract #3**

Client Responsibilities. Client understands that Service Provider is not an employee, and this will be a collaborative, professional relationship of equals where mutual professional respect, courtesy, and consideration are expected. Due to the virtual nature of the relationship, Client understands the importance of communication, especially via email, and agrees to respond to questions, requests, and communications from Service Provider in a timely manner. Timely manner will be defined and agreed upon by both parties. Client understands that Service Provider is a business with other clients to service, and requires fair, realistic notice to attend to requests and projects. Poor planning or miscommunication on the part of Client will not constitute an emergency for the Service Provider. Client understands that Service Provider may require detailed clarifications of projects to meet expectations and provide the best support and highest-quality work.

Office Hours and Communication. Office hours are Monday through Friday from 9 A.M. to 5 P.M. [Insert Time Zone]. Email is to be the primary form of communication between Client and Service Provider. Service Provider is available for phone calls during office hours only. Duration of phone calls will be billed as service hours. Telephone meetings must be prescheduled. Cancelation requires 12 hours advance notice. Missed meetings or cancelations without sufficient notice will be billed to the client.

Service Provider guarantees a two-hour virtual "nod" or acknowledgment of communication from the Client. This does not ensure completion of a task within two hours, but will ensure consistent and predictable communication between Service Provider and Client.

Project Completion. Basic administrative support receives 24- to 48-hour attention. Each new or special project requires a minimum of three days' lead time. Client will provide sufficient notice and allow for reasonable time frames for project completion. Rush projects of 24 hours or less and projects requiring weekend or holiday work will be subject to a 50 percent surcharge. Service Provider reserves the right to refuse any project service requested.

Client will provide all content, outlines, images, and other information necessary for any special projects.

Expenses. Expenses incurred on behalf of the Client not included in any fees will be billed to the Client. Reimbursable expenses include, but are not limited to: office

FIGURE 7–3: **Sample Freelance Employment Contract #3,** continued

supplies, mileage, long-distance telephone charges, payments made to vendors, and shipping and handling costs. On-site visits will be billed for hourly time, time spent traveling, and mileage. Payment is due upon receipt.

Accuracy. Client assumes full responsibility for acceptance of work or services performed and agreed upon, as well as final proofing and accuracy.

Payment Options. Payments are accepted via [Insert Payment Method(s)].

Late Payments. Payments not received by due date may result in work cessation. Service Provider reserves the right to refuse completion or delivery of work until past due balances are paid. Late payments will incur a $25 late fee.

Property. All billings (including invoices, statements, and estimates), reports, and time accounting are provided as a convenience to Client at the discretion of Service Provider and remain the property of Service Provider. Periodic audits may reveal previous billing discrepancies or errors, and Service Provider is entitled to void or recall incorrect invoices and statements and bill for any monies due on account.

Accuracy of Information. Client agrees that the accuracy of information supplied to Service Provider is the sole responsibility of Client and that Service Provider is not responsible and shall not be held liable for the result of services performed on the basis of inaccurate, incomplete, or untruthful information furnished by the Client.

Termination. Retainers may be terminated by either party for any reason with 10 (ten) days' advance notice of intent to cancel. Retainer fees are due in full for the intended month of cancelation if proper notice is not provided.

Expiration and Modification. This agreement shall remain in effect until such time as one or the other party provides written notice of cancelation. This agreement may be modified or amended as necessary after negotiations initiated by either party. If agreement is reached, only a written instrument signed by both parties will modify or amend this agreement.

Governing Law. This agreement shall be governed by, construed, and enforced in accordance with the laws of the State of [Your State Here]. If any part of this agreement is adjudged as invalid, illegal, or unenforceable, the remaining parts shall not be affected and remain in full force and effect.

FIGURE 7–3: **Sample Freelance Employment Contract #3,** continued

Notices. Any notice provided for or concerning this agreement shall be in writing and shall be deemed sufficiently given when sent by certified or registered mail if sent to the respective address of each party as set forth in this agreement.

WITNESS our signatures as of the day and date first above stated.

_____   _____
(Name of Service Provider)   (Name of Client)

By: _____   By: _____
(Printed Name and Office in Corporation)   (Printed Name and Office in Corporation)

_____   _____
(Signature of Officer)   (Date)   (Signature of Officer)   (Date)

FIGURE 7–3: **Sample Freelance Employment Contract #3,** continued

Sample Virtual Assistant Employment Contract

Thank you for getting started with [Company]. You are mere moments away from augmenting your team and scaling your agency. Please enter the following billing information so we can setup your profile.

First Name of Billing Contact	
Last Name of Billing Contact	
Company/Organization	
Billing Address	
Billing City	
Billing State	
Billing ZIP	
Phone Number of Billing Contact	
Email of Billing Contact	

I authorize [Company] to electronically debit my bank account or credit card for all fees incurred according to the terms outlined below. I acknowledge that electronic debits against my account must comply with United States law. All charges are automatically billed at the beginning of each month for charges incurred during the prior month. This payment authorization is to remain in effect until I notify [Company] of cancelation by giving written notice in enough time for the business and receiving financial institution to have a reasonable opportunity to act on it.

Please Choose and Complete One of the Following Payment Methods

ACH (U.S. Banks Only)

Name on Bank Account	
Bank Account Type	
Bank Routing Number	
Bank Account Number	

FIGURE 7–4: **Sample Freelance Employment Contract #4**

Credit Card

Name on Credit Card	
Credit Card Number	
Credit Card Expiration Date	
Card Verification Code (CVV)	

I have completed one of the payment methods above: _____

_____   _____

Billable Time. I understand that [Company] team members track billable time for all work done for my agency or any communication between [Company] and (or on behalf of) my agency. This includes (but may not be limited to) production work, internal communication related to my work or my agency, email (or Slack, etc.) correspondence, meetings and consultations with me or other members of my agency's team, discussions of work details and scope, research time and time spent on estimates, and all time spent related to work done for my agency or general correspondence between [Company] and my agency.

Initial _____   _____

Real-Time Reporting. I understand that I have access to a dashboard that provides real-time reports of the time spent on my work as well as a running total of charges pending. I understand that I can log in anytime and see the current balance and details of the work that has been performed.

Initial _____   _____

Terms & Conditions. By entering your payment information and completing this form, you are agreeing to the following terms and conditions between [Company] and you or your company ("Client"):

Services for a given month will be billed via a single Invoice on or around the first day of the following month and will be charged to the credit card or bank account on file.

FIGURE 7–4: **Sample Freelance Employment Contract #4,** continued

Pricing has been disclosed to and accepted by Client during the sales call between Client and [Company] through email.

By submitting this form, you authorize [Company] to bill your credit card or bank account for any charges incurred during the course of doing business with [Company]. This authorization will remain in effect until it is canceled in writing. You certify that you are an authorized user of this credit card/bank account and will not dispute these scheduled transactions with your bank or credit card company as long as the transactions correspond to the terms indicated in the course of normal business with [Company].

The hours billed are based upon Client's discretion. Client has the ability to log into an online portal for real-time updates of Client's usage of [Company] services, and by submitting this form is indicating that the transactions correspond to the terms indicated in the normal course of business with [Company].

The relationship of the Parties hereunder is that of independent contractors, and nothing in these terms and conditions or any other communications between [Company] and Client is intended to, or shall be construed to, create a partnership, agency, joint venture, employment, or similar relationship. It is the understanding and intention of Client and [Company] that in the performance of any Work by [Company] for Client, [Company] and its employees, agents, or representatives shall be deemed to be an independent contractor of Client. Nothing contained in these terms and conditions or any other communications between [Company] and Client will be construed to be inconsistent with such independent contractor relationship.

Client understands and agrees that [Company] has invested time, expenses, and resources in training, orienting, and equipping its employees with the knowledge and experience to perform their duties. Therefore, Client shall not, during the period in which [Company] provides services for Client, or at any time within two (2) years thereafter, retain or employ any current or former [Company] employee who worked for [Company] during the [Company]-Client relationship on a full-time, part-time, project basis, or in any other capacity as an independent contractor, employee, or consultant. If Client does so, it agrees to pay [Company] a permanent placement fee equal to 20 percent of the first-year gross compensation of the employee as offered by the Client. Client and [Company] agree that it would be extremely difficult or impossible to ascertain the actual amount in which [Company]

FIGURE 7–4: **Sample Freelance Employment Contract #4,** continued

would be damaged by such actions by Client and accordingly agree that these liquidated damages in the form of the personal placement fee are reasonable.

NEITHER PARTY WILL BE LIABLE TO THE OTHER FOR LOST PROFITS OR LOST BUSINESS, INDIRECT, CONSEQUENTIAL, OR PUNITIVE DAMAGES, WHETHER BASED IN CONTRACT OR TORT (INCLUDING NEGLIGENCE, STRICT LIABILITY, OR OTHERWISE), WHETHER OR NOT EITHER PARTY HAS BEEN ADVISED OF THE POSSIBILITY OF SUCH DAMAGES. IN THE EVENT OF ANY LIABILITY FROM [Company] TO CLIENT ARISING FROM THE BUSINESS RELATIONSHIP BETWEEN THE PARTIES, [Company's] TOTAL LIABILITY TO CLIENT WILL BE LIMITED TO CLIENT'S ACTUAL DIRECT DAMAGES, NOT TO EXCEED THE AGGREGATE AMOUNT PAID BY CLIENT TO [Company] DURING THE TWELVE (12) MONTH PERIOD PRECEDING THE EVENT FROM WHICH THE DAMAGES AROSE.

The person agreeing to these terms and conditions represents that he or she has full and legal authority to execute this agreement for and on behalf of Client and to bind Client.

Name: _____

Title:_____

Signature: _____

Date: _____

FIGURE 7–4: **Sample Freelance Employment Contract #4,** continued

Managing Your Time and Work-Related Tools

You know that old saying "Time is money"? For a virtual assistant, nothing could be truer. If you're not actively spending time handling tasks and projects for your clients, you're not getting paid. The more you can get done, the more money you make. How much you're able to do during any given day will greatly depend on your time management and organizational skills. You can augment these skills, however, with the proper tools to enhance your efficiency.

Time Management Basics

If you haven't yet mastered effective time management, you'll likely need to modify your behavior and work habits. Perhaps the first lesson you should learn about time management is never to overcommit yourself.

Before taking on any work, determine how many hours per day or week you'll be able to dedicate to being a virtual assistant. After subtracting the time you need to devote to managing your business, determine how much time is left to handle client-related activities.

If this works out to six hours per day, for example, evaluate everything that needs to be done during that time. With practice, you'll get to know how much you can realistically get done in a workday. Don't commit to tackling more than this, or you'll wind up needing to work longer hours and eventually burn out.

Each day, based on your upcoming deadlines and client demands, prioritize each activity and estimate how long it will take. Classify each task or activity as:

> *Top priority*. Something that must be completed by a specific time that day. (It has a firm deadline.)
> *High priority*. Something that needs to be completed by the end of that day.
> *Normal priority*. Something that should get done that day, but could be pushed to the following day, if necessary.
> *Low priority*. Something that should get done within the next few days but has no pressing deadline.

Estimate the amount of time each task or activity will take to complete, and keep a detailed record of which client each is associated with.

At the very end of each workday, take a few minutes to plan out your next day, or do this the first thing each morning. Divide your day into 15-minute increments with a calendar, project management app, to-do list, or

> **tip** ⓘ
>
> Assign a visual icon (or symbol) and a color to each priority level for quick and easy visualization as you review your daily schedule/calendar. For example, four red stars (****) could indicate top priority tasks. Three yellow stars (***) could mean high priority tasks, two blue stars (**) could be normal priority tasks, and one green star (*) could be low priority tasks. Come up with a system that works for you.

scheduling app (depending on your work habits and which organizational tool works best for you).

Plan to get the most important items or tasks on your list done first, so schedule these in the morning. If you have time left at the end of your workday, this is when you should work on any remaining low priority tasks. Should these items not get done, push them to the next day, but boost them from low priority to normal priority if necessary.

To further enhance your time management skills, get to know your personal limits. For example, consider the following questions:

▶ How much time can you spend doing a particular task before your mind goes numb, you lose interest, or you're no longer able to focus?

▶ How often will you benefit from taking a 15-minute break during your workday? Be sure to schedule regular downtime into your workday. Get up from your desk, leave your office, and take a quick walk or go to the kitchen and make yourself a cup of coffee.

▶ How much time should you allocate for lunch to maintain peak performance throughout the afternoon? Some people thrive on a 15-minute lunch break, while others need an hour to eat, clear their head, and regroup before starting their afternoon.

Another consideration when planning your daily schedule involves your circadian rhythm. During what times of the day are your mind and body at peak performance level? Are you unable to fully concentrate on tasks first thing in the morning? Does your mind become fatigued after 4 P.M.? Based on your patterns, avoid scheduling top or high priority items when you know you won't be at peak efficiency levels.

Anytime you're working on top priority or high priority tasks or activities, your mind and body should be at highest efficiency, or you'll likely find yourself working more slowly, making more mistakes, and doing subpar work that will ultimately have a negative impact on your productivity.

Remember, in addition to all the tasks and activities you must do for your clients, there will be at least a

tip

As you study your work habits and productivity throughout the day, learn how to identify signs of frustration, fatigue, and inattentiveness. Discover how to overcome these feelings before they become overwhelming. A quick deep breathing exercise, a five-minute meditation activity, or a few sips of coffee, for example, might get you through a particularly rough patch in your day. Learn to identify and address your needs throughout your workday in the most efficient and healthiest way possible.

handful of important tasks you need to complete to keep your business running smoothly. Don't consistently leave these items until the end of your workday, when you're fatigued and unable to give each task the attention it deserves.

Obviously, unexpected things happen. A task will take longer than you thought it would, you'll be contacted by a client about an emergency, or your internet service will go down for a few hours. Being able to quickly adjust your schedule to accommodate the unexpected is another skill you'll need to develop and ultimately master.

Anytime a delay happens or problem arises, keep your clients apprised. Maintain realistic expectations about how deadlines may need to be adjusted and keep the lines of communication flowing with periodic updates to your clients.

Don't Overextend Yourself

One of the worst time management mistakes you can make is taking on too much work. As you analyze your schedule, don't accept work you know you won't be able to complete on time.

By accepting all work that's offered to you, you may think you're helping your clients, or you may be focusing on how much money you can make, but overworking yourself will lead to problems like burnout, missed deadlines, and disgruntled clients.

Instead of assuring your client that a project will get done by an unrealistic deadline you already know you can't meet, be honest. Explain that your schedule is booked solid and then discuss realistic deadlines for completing the new work.

Prioritize Your Clients Fairly

Depending on how you bill your clients, you should prioritize tasks or activities from clients who have you on a retainer, a long-term contract, or who have prepaid for a large block of your time that week (or month). These are the people who generate most of your income, and you need to keep them happy, as opposed to a client who offers a short-term project with no long-term income or business relationship potential.

Giving priority to clients you simply like more (on a personal level) is not good business practice. But clients you have a long-term and ongoing relationship with should be given priority attention.

Sometimes You May Want or Need to Turn Down Work

If you're asked to handle something that you don't know how to do, or will take you too long to learn, or you will absolutely hate doing, remember it's OK to say "no" to a client (or prospective client) and turn down the work. Obviously, you should decide this on a case-by-case basis, taking the quality of your client's relationship and history with you into account.

There will be times when, to deal with client emergencies, you will need to work more hours to get everything done. This is the reality of owning your own business. If you're having to do this every day, or every week, however, it's a sign you're taking on too much work or need to tweak your time management process.

At the end of every week, take a few minutes to analyze how you spent every hour of every day. Look for blocks of time where you were focused on unimportant, mundane, or

► Every Minute Counts!

Knowing what you need to get done each day and actually accomplishing those objectives are an essential part of time management. As a virtual assistant who works with multiple clients, however, an equally important part is keeping track of how much time you spend on each task or activity—down to the minute—so you can bill each client appropriately.

For this, you'll want to invest and become proficient in using a powerful time tracker. Software packages designed specifically for VAs, like Adminja and HoneyBook, have a time tracker module built in that allows you to manage multiple activities and clients simultaneously. There are also plenty of stand-alone applications for Windows PCs, Macs, and mobile devices that can help you with accurate time tracking.

Select a time tracker that accommodates your work habits and needs. You'll likely need to provide detailed daily, weekly, and/or monthly reports to each client describing exactly what you did for them and how much time (again, down to the minute) you dedicated to each task or activity. A good time tracker app will allow you to create these reports very quickly without needing to do any calculations or formatting.

As you jump from task to task, don't forget to turn the appropriate time trackers on and off. This is a habit you'll need to practice initially, as you get used to handling tasks for multiple clients throughout each workday.

There may be times when you're inclined to give extra, unbilled time to a client. Don't do this too often or clients will come to expect it, and it will have a negative impact on your profit margin. Just giving away ten minutes of your time to six different clients means you worked an hour without making any money. Your time is valuable, and you shouldn't be expected to work for free.

busy work-related tasks that ultimately proved to be a waste of time. Once you identify these activities, consider delegating them to your own, low-cost VA so they don't wind up wasting time you could be using to bill clients.

If tasks like managing your email inbox or generating reports for clients are taking up five hours per week, for example, hiring a VA to handle them might cost you $10 to $15 per hour (or between $50 and $75 per week). However, if doing this creates five additional hours in your schedule for client work that you bill out at $75 per hour, that's $375 in extra income (and $300 per week in profit after paying your VA). It also means you won't have to do these tasks yourself, so you can focus more on the work you enjoy and are good at.

20 Additional Tips for Mastering Time Management

The following are a collection of proven time management tips and strategies. Remember, if your clients can't rely on you to complete your work on time and in a way that meets or exceeds their expectations, they'll likely find a different VA or have the work done in-house instead. This will tarnish your reputation and negatively impact your bottom line.

Pick and choose the strategies from this list that best fit your existing work habits.

1. When you have a large project or task, whenever possible, divide it up into a series of smaller, more achievable objectives and list those within a separate to-do list. As you complete each mini-objective, check it off your list. With each added checkmark, you'll feel a sense of accomplishment and be one step closer to completing the larger project or task. Be sure to associate a deadline with each mini-objective.

2. Anytime you set a goal for yourself, make sure it's realistic, specific, measurable, and attainable. By associating your goals with deadlines, you'll know what you need to achieve and when. This should help keep you motivated and focused.

3. As you juggle a variety of tasks and activities throughout your day for a handful of different clients, take a short break (5 to 15 minutes) between each so you can clear your head and refocus on the next task.

tip

If you can't break the habit of constantly visiting pointless websites, browsing online shopping sites, and checking social media accounts while using your computer, install an application, such as SelfControl (https://selfcontrolapp.com) or Freedom (https://freedom.to), which will block these sites and services during your defined business hours.

4. Avoid the biggest distractions and time wasters, like checking your social media feeds, constantly checking your email inbox, texting friends, or making personal calls.

5. Study your own work habits to determine what works best for you and how to maximize your work flow with no burnout. This means knowing what times of day you're most alert and efficient, understanding the best way for you to juggle multiple tasks without losing focus, and learning how to avoid procrastination when you're working from home and nobody is supervising or motivating you.

6. Determine the best ways to handle the tasks and responsibilities associated with running your own business.

7. Provide yourself with a comprehensive arsenal of powerful software tools that will help you meet your responsibilities in the most efficient way possible. Your goal should be to use technology to improve your communication, speed up and streamline your work flow, manage key tasks and responsibilities, and make sure the information you need is secure yet readily accessible on all your computers and mobile devices.

8. As you begin work on a new project or task, anticipate what problems might arise. Come up with an action plan for dealing with them in advance, so if something does go wrong, you won't waste time panicking or having to figure out what to do. You'll already have a game plan and procedure in place.

9. Take advantage of tools to help you organize your paperwork and digital files. While Windows PCs and Macs (as well as mobile devices) have a universal search tool built into the operating system, properly naming files and placing them in properly named folders and subfolders, for example, will make things much easier to locate.

10. Don't procrastinate and wait for an important deadline to approach because you feel you work better under pressure. You're better off finishing a task early than rushing to get it done on time. Rushing could result in mistakes or inferior work.

11. Instead of constantly checking and responding to incoming emails and text messages, set aside specific times each day to do this. If a client needs to reach you urgently, develop a plan for what they should do to get your attention, such as a phone call.

12. Don't drag out meetings with clients. Go into each meeting or phone call with a preset agenda and a chosen duration. Most phone calls or video calls/virtual meetings should not need to last more than 15 minutes unless its specific agenda requires more of everyone's time.

13. Once your workday is over, turn on the "Do Not Disturb" feature on your computer, smartphone, and work-related messaging services (such as Slack).

14. Take online classes, read how-to books, or take advantage of other training opportunities to become highly proficient at all the software tools you're required to use, both in your own business and with clients. This will save you a lot of time and frustration trying to figure out how to use features and functions you need, especially when you're working under a tight deadline.

15. Organize your email inbox and take advantage of a customizable spam filter. Create separate folders for incoming messages, labeled "Urgent," "Unimportant," and "Needs Further Action," for example. You can also customize your email software to sort incoming messages based on recipient or keyword. For emails that require a common or generic response, pre-write those canned responses and send them out as needed to save time.

> **tip**
>
> If you do get stuck trying to figure out something, seek out a tutorial on YouTube. For example, if you need to quickly discover how to format a Microsoft Word document into three columns, enter "How do I create a three-column document in Microsoft Word?" in the YouTube search field. The search results will likely reveal a handful of short videos that can answer your question.

16. Avoid multitasking. Instead of trying to get multiple things done at once, focus on and complete one task at a time, and then move on to the next. For example, if you're on a business phone call, don't simultaneously check your email.

17. Set a timer for each task or activity you embark on. If you're working under a time constraint, you're more apt to get it done. If the timer reaches zero and you're not finished, you can either extend the timer by an additional predetermined amount of time or return to the task later, depending on its level of importance.

18. Set up an efficient work space or office in your home, and keep your work habits consistent. Everything you need to get your work done should be within arm's reach in your home office. If you need a paper clip, for example, you shouldn't have to leave the room and search for one.

19. Prepare for the unexpected when it comes to technology. It's not a matter of *if* your computer or mobile device will someday crash or break—it's *when*. In addition to maintaining secure local and cloud-based backups of your data, have a

plan in place for if you temporarily lose power or your internet or phone line stops working. Consider investing in an uninterruptible power supply for your computer and getting a smartphone service plan with a 5G wifi hotspot feature you can connect your computer(s) to if your home internet goes down. Being ready for breakdowns will speed up your recovery time and eliminate a lot of unnecessary hassle and stress.

20. Make sure you and your client both understand what the words "urgent" and "emergency" mean. If something seems important but is not actually urgent or an emergency, don't drop everything else to deal with it. Instead, just schedule that new task into your day.

▶ Stay Up-to-Date on the Latest Tools and Online Collaboration Trends

Thanks to the rapid evolution of technology, whatever software you choose will get regular updates, with new features and functions constantly being added. At the same time, the tools your clients rely on will likely change over time. For example, prior to the Covid-19 pandemic, Zoom was not the most widely used virtual meeting and videoconferencing tool in the business world. As of early 2021, with more than 300 million active accounts, it's now by far one of the most popular.

As a virtual assistant, one of your ongoing responsibilities is to keep up with the latest advancements and updates to the tools you and your clients regularly use while staying informed about new applications that could improve the way you or your clients work.

Dedicate at least a few hours per month to research and training, so your proficiency at using the necessary software remains up-to-date. Keeping your data secure (password protected and encrypted), backed up (locally and in the cloud), and synchronized between all your computers and mobile devices will be essential to your efficiency, as will the ability to use the appropriate virtual collaboration tools to work with each client.

It's best to stick with tools that are widely used in business and that are compatible with the tools your clients use. These days, compatibility between Windows PCs and Macs, for example, is no longer an obstacle. However, when you and your clients are using different versions of the same application, or different applications that claim to be able to seamlessly share information, file or data compatibility issues often arise.

Common Collaboration and Productivity Tools That'll Help You Save Time

Whether you're billing clients by the hour or on a per-project basis, how you spend your time will determine your income. Developing top-notch time management skills is essential. However, to maximize your productivity, you'll need to use the right tools for the job.

While some developers have tried to provide all-in-one software solutions for virtual assistants and/or small businesses, even if you decide to use one of these tools, you'll likely need additional apps to handle all your tasks and responsibilities, while maintaining compatibility and easy accessibility with each of your clients.

As you develop your own arsenal of software tools that will help you become the best virtual assistant possible, you'll likely need to learn (or at least familiarize yourself with) many widely used applications. For example, you may prefer Zoom for virtual meetings, but some of your clients might use GoToMeeting, Skype, or Microsoft Teams. Thus, you'll need to become familiar with each of these services to properly communicate with all your clients.

> **tip** ⓘ
>
> The time you invest upfront into becoming and staying proficient at using specific tools will ultimately save you a lot of time later trying to figure things out when you're working under a tight deadline. These time wasters might include learning how to use a new feature or function that is essential for completing a task, fixing a time-consuming mistake, or dealing with connectivity, compatibility, security, or synchronization issues.

Always Use the Right Tool for the Job

There is a vast selection of software options available, so choose the ones that best meet your needs. You should not have to compromise or adjust your work habits or work flow to fit the application. Instead, find a tool that can be personalized or customized to meet your needs.

With the exception of the tools you're required to use to accommodate your clients, before integrating any application or tool into your work flow, determine:

- ► What it's supposed to do
- ► The purchase or subscription cost (if you buy it outright, will there be an upgrade fee whenever a new version is released?)
- ► The time investment it will take to set up and learn to use it
- ► What free or low-cost training and technical support will be available

- ▶ How it will help you save time or become more efficient and productive
- ▶ What problem(s) or challenge(s) it will help you overcome
- ▶ Whether it needs to synchronize or share information with other applications you already use
- ▶ If it will keep your data secure
- ▶ What problems you may encounter in conjunction with its implementation
- ▶ If you'll be able to replace or phase out other tools or applications you currently use once you implement it

Focus on Security Today and Save a Lot of Time Moving Forward

One of the things you'll need to guarantee your clients is confidentiality, because you'll likely be dealing with their trade secrets and other proprietary information that's not public knowledge (and that should not fall into the hands of their competitors).

In addition to being an honorable and trustworthy person in all your business dealings, it's also necessary to ensure the technology and tools you use are as secure as possible.

Investing the time to secure your business from the start will save you a lot of time, money, and frustration, as well as protect your professional reputation and credibility.

Keep in mind that one of the biggest causes of data breaches, online fraud, and identity theft in the business world is human error. This includes sharing the wrong data with the wrong people; accidentally revealing passwords to unauthorized people; and making foolish mistakes that make it easier to hack computers, networks, cloud-based accounts, mobile devices, and/or applications.

Password Security and Management Are a Must

Start by adding password security to all your computers and mobile devices. This feature is built into the Windows, Mac OS, iOS, and Android operating systems; you should make sure to turn it on and fully use it.

Next, turn on two-factor authorization on all software that supports it, including your cloud-based file sharing/data backup service. You'll also want to use

fun fact ☺

Check out this list of the 200 most frequently used passwords of 2020 published by NordPass (https://nordpass.com/most-common-passwords-list), and then make sure none of your passwords are featured on this or any similar list.

different passwords for each of your accounts and select passwords that are not obvious or commonly used. ("Password" is one of the most widely used passwords in the world.)

Seriously consider using a password manager to create and manage a comprehensive and secure database of all your account-related passwords. These applications sync your password database between all your computers and mobile devices but keep it encrypted and password protected. You only have to remember one password—the one that opens the password manager. Choose a password manager that supports all your computers and mobile devices; most have versions for Windows, Mac OS, iOS, and Android.

Popular password managers include:

▶ 1Password: https://1password.com
▶ Dashlane: https://www.dashlane.com/
▶ Keeper: https://www.keepersecurity.com/
▶ LastPass: https://www.lastpass.com/
▶ NordPass: https://nordpass.com

An alternative to a password manager is a hardware-based password key, such as Everykey (https://everykey.com).

According to the company's website, "Everykey has a variety of safety features that work together to keep your information safe. Everykey utilizes four layers of AES 128-bit, AES 256-bit, and RSA 4096-bit encryption, and has remote freezing capabilities which prevent others from using your Everykey in the event that it is lost or stolen."

Every time Everykey sends an encrypted Bluetooth Low Energy message, its contents are changed. This prevents a hacker from spoofing an Everykey. Keep in mind that device passwords are never stored on an Everykey server or product. All these features work together to make Everykey a secure and safer tool.

Add Security and Privacy Extensions to Your Web Browser

When it comes to web browsers, be sure to manually turn on and adjust the browser's built-in security features. For example, if you're using Google Chrome, access the Chrome menu and select the Preferences menu, then from the Settings menu, select the Safety Check option, followed by the Privacy and Security option.

Using third-party web browser extensions (also called plug-ins), you can add further security and privacy features when using a Windows PC or Mac. To access a directory of optional free and fee-based extensions, visit:

▶ Apple Safari: From the App Store, select the Safari Extensions category.
▶ Google Chrome: https://chrome.google.com/webstore/category/extensions

▶ Microsoft Edge: https://microsoftedge.microsoft.com/addons/Microsoft-Edge-Extensions-Home

▶ Mozilla Firefox: https://addons.mozilla.org/en-US/firefox/extensions

Take Advantage of a Virtual Private Network for Added Security

Yet another important way to protect your security (and the security of your clients) is to install a virtual private network (VPN) application on each of your computers and mobile devices and make sure it's activated anytime you're connected to the internet through wifi (including your home wifi network or any public wifi connection when you're on the go).

A VPN will automatically encrypt all data coming and going from your computer or mobile device, make your location impossible to determine, and help eliminate ad trackers and other technologies that a hacker could use to steal your data.

Choose a VPN from a widely known company that offers many servers, such as:

▶ CyberGhost VPN: https://www.cyberghostvpn.com/

▶ ExpressVPN: https://www.expressvpn.com/

▶ McAfee VPN: https://www.mcafee.com/en-us/vpn.html

▶ NordVPN: https://nordvpn.com

▶ Norton VPN: https://us.norton.com/products/norton-secure-vpn

▶ Private Internet Access: https://www.privateinternetaccess.com/

Turn On the Password and Security Features in the Applications You Use

Many office suites (including Microsoft Office, Microsoft 365, and Google Workspace), as well as PDF file creators (including Adobe Acrobat and PDFCreator) and bookkeeping applications (including QuickBooks), allow you to add password protection to individual files. This is a useful tool when creating documents that you will be sharing or collaborating on with others, and that contain confidential or proprietary information.

There are also security tools built into all virtual meeting and messaging applications, for example, that you should be sure to activate. However, in addition to adding security precautions to everything you do digitally, your activities in the real world can also impact client security and privacy.

Get into the habit of shredding (not just throwing away) paper documents that relate to your clients, as well as your own financial records that are ready to be discarded. When speaking on the phone with clients outside your home office, make sure nobody is around and potentially eavesdropping.

A little common sense and taking advantage of security tools (including the features already built into your computers, mobile devices, and applications) will go a long way toward preventing criminals from gaining access to data from your business and your clients.

Seek Out a Mentor

Being able to work with, be trained by, or obtain advice from an experienced mentor will be extremely valuable as you launch and begin to manage your virtual assistant business. Seek out someone you respect and trust, and who is willing to help you succeed.

In the meantime, the next chapter features a collection of interviews with well-established and successful virtual assistants who share advice, tips, and strategies based on their real-world experiences. Some of this information you might not agree with, or it might not pertain directly to you. However, from all these interviews, you'll gain valuable insight into a wide range of subjects related to achieving long-term success as a virtual assistant.

Experienced VAs Share Their Thoughts and Advice

If you're still wondering what it takes to succeed as a virtual assistant, or you have questions about what it's really like to be a virtual assistant who caters to multiple clients, there's no better place to turn than to a handful of independent, experienced, and successful VAs.

Through these in-depth and exclusive interviews, you'll learn the thoughts and opinions of virtual assistants who have overcome mistakes, pioneered new ways to do things, discovered how to make their services appealing to clients, and harnessed their unique skill sets, personality traits, education, and work experience to transform themselves into successful business operators in the ever-evolving virtual assistant industry.

tip

Moving forward, seriously look into finding a mentor—someone who will work with you one-on-one and cater their advice specifically to you and your business.

The people interviewed here come from vastly different backgrounds and focus on different niches in the VA field. Each shares advice for up-and-coming virtual assistants who hope to follow in their footsteps. While you may not agree with their opinion about a specific topic or plan to pursue a different niche for your business, chances are you'll still gain valuable insight into how you too can become a successful virtual assistant.

David Hogan, Throne Consulting

David Hogan has been working as an executive assistant for more than 17 years. He gained experience working for CEOs and top-level executives at companies of all sizes and in a variety of industries. After spending so much time in the corporate world, he discovered an increasing need for independent and highly skilled executive assistants who can work remotely. Once the Covid-19 pandemic started to impact the corporate world, he chose to pursue working as an independent virtual assistant on a full-time basis.

How did you decide becoming a virtual assistant would be a good fit for you?

David Hogan: My story is a bit different from most other people. I never went to college and consider myself to be self-taught. My career started with a job at a call center, so I figured I'd wind up as a customer service manager or call center manager. When the former executive assistant at the call center suddenly left the company, the owner came to me and asked if I'd like to become his new executive assistant. Now, almost two decades later, one of the main things that attracted me to become a virtual assistant is the flexible work schedule. I wanted to be able to control my own work-life balance at this point in my career.

How do the day-to-day responsibilities differ between what you formerly did as an executive assistant and what you do now as a virtual assistant who caters to top-level business leaders?

Hogan: The work itself, in terms of the tasks I do every day to support my executive clients, has changed very little. A few years ago, few people working in the corporate world believed that someone working remotely from their home could accomplish the same level of work as someone working in a traditional corporate office, but that's no longer the case. The biggest change for me is that I am now also in charge of all aspects related to running my own business.

How do you define the role of a virtual assistant? What does the job title mean to you?

Hogan: Many top-level executives I talk to are only first starting to open their minds regarding how they could benefit from hiring an experienced virtual assistant. Many believe the scope of what a virtual assistant can do for them is limited to things like calendar management and inbox management. I believe a virtual assistant, especially one with more than 18 years' worth of experience, can do anything a traditional executive assistant can do. Over the years, I have acquired many skills, and have successfully completed so many different types of tasks, that working remotely, I am able to quickly adapt and accommodate just about any need a client might have.

How important is it for a VA to brand themselves and their company?

Hogan: I would say branding is pretty important. Most VAs don't have the work experience that I do and can offer a much narrower selection of services. My branding emphasizes my experience and the ways I can benefit a top-level executive while saving them money by not having to hire a full-time employee and incur all the costs associated with that.

Because I can do so much more than a typical administrative assistant or virtual assistant, I created a series of one-page documents that explain some of the core services I can provide. I use these documents to compare what a typical VA can do vs. what I can do for a client. Defining how I am different, and spelling it out for my prospective clients, is the basis of my brand.

I always tell my clients that if they are not sure I can handle a specific task or responsibility, they should ask. Chances are, having worked so closely with so many different top-level executives for almost two decades, I have probably done something just like their request before.

What would you say are the most important personality traits a virtual assistant must have to succeed?

Hogan: You definitely need to be someone who can multitask and handle a wide range of personalities. When you're working so closely with a variety of people, you'll need to deal with them when they're happy, upset, uncertain, and frustrated, so you'll be exposed to a lot of raw emotion that will be directed toward you, but have absolutely nothing to do with you. Having a thick skin is important. Being energetic and outgoing are also useful personality traits, because as a virtual assistant, you may be called upon to serve as a confidant to your clients. When they are frustrated and upset, you'll need to be confident, cool, and collected, so you can support them and guide them as needed.

When you're first getting started as a VA, don't initially say no to work you may not be qualified for. Do some research and learn what it'll take to complete the task or project, and then make an educated decision about whether you can handle it successfully without letting down your client. If you can handle it, you'll be expanding your skill set, which will make you more marketable in the future. Taking on new types of work forces you to learn new skills, which will help keep the job interesting and challenging.

When you decided to transition from the corporate world to becoming an independent virtual assistant, how did you land your first few clients?

Hogan: I decided to focus on startups so I can use my experience to cater to the needs of executives first learning how to do what it takes to make their new business successful. I initially tried using many different social media services to market myself, but I ultimately discovered that for me, LinkedIn worked best as a powerful networking tool for finding prospective new clients.

For example, using LinkedIn, I will research businesses and then do a cold reach out to the company's president or CEO with a simple message that explains who I am and my qualifications. I then state that if they need advice on how to utilize virtual support, they should let me know. I quickly landed nine major clients with this simple technique. My approach on LinkedIn is to be personable and human, without trying to shove a sales pitch down someone's throat. My core marketing message is, "When you need me, I am here to support you."

Executives are probably accustomed to having their assistant give them their full attention, but when they hire you as a virtual assistant, you need to juggle their needs along with the needs of your other clients. How does that work from a scheduling standpoint?

Hogan: The clients that prepurchase a block of my time every month get the highest priority. Of course, I don't take on work I know I don't have time to do, so it's just a matter of prioritizing what needs to be done and when. The people who book me by the hour, on an as-needed basis, know that I will get to their work as soon as possible, but I won't drop everything else to accommodate their sense of urgency.

For the clients who hire me for blocks of time or on a retainer, I will have a conversation with them about what time of day they need my attention. For example, if they need a four-hour block of time every Monday to complete a specific and timely task, I can typically accommodate that if they request it in advance. One of my initial conversations during the client onboarding process is discussing what the client wants my support to look like from a scheduling standpoint.

Since you work primarily with startups and you have so much experience, does the client typically dictate what they need, or do you inform the client about what they should be using you for?

Hogan: It's a combination of both. When someone first comes to me, they often think they understand what they need, but when we have a conversation, they often don't have realistic expectations about what's possible and in what time frame, so I explain the most productive ways they can utilize my time. I never push too hard, but I will offer guidance when it's requested.

What equipment and software do you rely on the most as a virtual assistant?

Hogan: I have a really high-end, reliable Windows-based laptop computer. I also use a Samsung tablet for taking handwritten notes. To communicate with my clients, I am available by phone, but most of them prefer using Zoom or Slack, for example. My goal is to discover what systems my client uses, and then I set myself up to work with those systems. My clients will typically set me up as a user of their applicable accounts or tools. Some of my clients also use Asana or Trello. For the operation of my virtual assistant business, I rely on HubSpot to handle CRM and QuickBooks for invoicing and accounting.

What tips can you offer about how to deal with difficult or overly demanding clients?

Hogan: Never walk into a conversation with a difficult client without first having come up with several potential solutions for whatever problem they're currently facing. Create solutions based on the personality of the client, not just your own knowledge and experience. If you provide several potential solutions, your client won't feel like you're pushing them to make a specific decision. I take a holistic approach to problem solving that involves guiding my clients, as opposed to telling them this is how to handle something.

Do you have any tips for managing your time and avoiding burnout?

Hogan: I always build at least three 30-minute breaks and a lunch break into my schedule every day. At the end of my day, I turn my computer off and leave my home office. I then focus on my personal life. If you don't develop the discipline to turn off and shut down at the end of your workday, you'll find yourself sitting in front of your computer until 11 P.M. every night, and you'll always be exhausted.

As you're starting out, come up with your normal hours of operation and determine if you want to be available to your clients on weekends and holidays. The work is always going to be there. Block out personal time and stick to your schedule. Of course, you may occasionally need to deal with client emergencies after hours or on weekends, but this should not be a regular occurrence. Set expectations about when and how quickly a client can expect to hear back from you, especially if they reach out after your normal hours.

What advice do you have about creating an employment contract between the virtual assistant and their client?

Hogan: When I first started out as a virtual assistant, I had a close friend who was already doing this, so she provided me with her boilerplate contract and other paperwork that I then customized. My contract is straightforward. I keep it very simple. I have a one-page document that goes along with the contract that explains what the contract means, how much it'll cost the client, what they're being locked into, and how much of my time they get. After reading the document and having a discussion, they already know what they're getting, so the contract can be simple. After the contract is signed, I provide a printed welcome kit that reiterates everything, including when I am available and what the client can expect from me.

Can you share advice about how to develop a long-term relationship with a client?

Hogan: I survey the clients regularly to make sure they're happy and that I am meeting or exceeding their expectations. During our regular calls, for example, I'll also bring up their future growth plans and discuss how I can help them achieve their goals. I try to establish an ongoing need for myself. I also offer a bonus for clients who provide referrals to me. For every referral that turns into a signed contract, I provide the referrer with $200 off their next invoice, which means they need to keep our relationship going to receive the discount. My clients have been very receptive to this.

Is there any other advice you can share with up-and-coming virtual assistants?

Hogan: The biggest piece of advice I wish someone had given me when I first started out is that it's OK to have potential clients not want to work with you. Don't ever take it personally. Develop a thick skin to deal with rejection. Don't try lowering your rates to gain a client that initially rejects you. Instead, focus on finding a more suitable client who will pay you what you're worth, benefit from working with you, and whom you'll enjoy working with.

Diana Ennen, Virtual Word Publishing

Diana Ennen is an accomplished author and a pioneer in the virtual assistant industry, which she's been working in since 1985. When she started, in the early days of the internet, she mainly handled word processing, bookkeeping, and medical and legal transcription from home. Most of her clients were local.

As the internet grew, she discovered she could adapt her skills to provide more virtual services, including marketing books for authors. Legal transcription continued to be in high demand, so she went back to school to get a paralegal degree. Over the years, Ennen has been active in several professional associations for virtual assistants, and through her marketing and promotional efforts, she often winds up with more work than she can handle.

What services do you typically offer as a virtual assistant today?

Diana Ennen: I offer clients a lot of PR and marketing services and media follow-up, especially for authors looking to promote their books in major media. I also use social media on behalf of my clients in a way that allows them to get more out of everything else they're doing from a marketing and promotional standpoint.

How do you define the role of a virtual assistant?

Ennen: The role of a virtual assistant has changed a lot over the years. Just a few years ago, people did not understand what a virtual assistant was. That has changed today. A virtual assistant is a partner in business whom the client can rely on, just as they'd rely on a valuable employee to handle specific tasks or projects.

I see my role as helping clients handle tasks they're not equipped to handle in-house, or that they don't have the time to handle properly. Once a VA finds the type of work they want to do, it's relatively easy to find clients that need that work done for them. I see this as a partnership.

A VA's job is to work together with the client to help them succeed. It's all about being that right hand to the client and helping them to become more successful. I get really involved with my clients and constantly work to build a trusting relationship with them. Clients need to feel comfortable that the work they assign to a VA will get done correctly and on time.

What are the most important traits a successful virtual assistant should possess?

Ennen: First and foremost, a virtual assistant needs to develop a true passion for the work they're doing and the clients they're doing it for. Through no fault of your own, there will be days when things go badly, and your passion will get you through them. You also need confidence and a belief in yourself. One of the primary responsibilities of a virtual assistant, if they want to grow their business and maintain interest in it, is to constantly be learning and working to expand their skill set. When people ask what you do, you need to be able to describe your skill set and qualifications clearly and succinctly. Brand yourself as someone who is an expert at performing the services you offer.

Through branding and messaging, be consistent across all your online platforms, including your website and social media accounts. By knowing who you are and what you can do, you'll be able to promote this to potential clients. Try to become well-known for doing work in your niche and make it known that you're good at what you do.

What tips can you offer an up-and-coming VA for finding and landing their first few clients?

Ennen: The best way to land your first clients will depend on the services you're providing. I have found that writing articles related to your areas of expertise, which explain to potential clients how to do something, will help you gain credibility and exposure. For example, I do book marketing, so I might write an article called "Five Tips for Book Marketing Success." If you can't get your articles published in the media, publish them yourself on your website or as part of a blog. Try to get yourself known as an expert.

Networking is another extremely powerful tool for finding and landing clients. Become active with industry associations that your prospective clients would likely be members of, and start hanging out, in the real world or online, with other virtual assistants. Often, if a VA is overbooked or asked to do something they're not comfortable with or qualified to do, they'll refer that work to another VA whom they know and trust. You could become that person.

Another way to find clients is to become active on special interest groups where you know your prospective clients will be active. Facebook groups and LinkedIn can be very useful for networking.

What advice can you offer about setting rates?

Ennen: There are a lot of virtual assistants who don't charge what they should be charging. Do your research and find out what the market for your services is. Some VAs list their pricing on their website, for example. This is a good place to start your research. Then, based on your skills and experience, come up with a fair rate. Don't lowball your pricing to undercut your competition. Most clients will have no trouble paying a competitive or even premium rate for the quality work you do if they have confidence in your ability to do the job right.

Do you believe in preselling clients a package or charging an hourly rate?

Ennen: It depends on the type of work you're doing and the types of clients you're catering to. Any of the different pricing models can work. It's just a matter of discovering what works best for what you're offering. I like to use a retainer model and then sell blocks of time. With a monthly retainer, the client guarantees they'll utilize a predetermined amount of the VA's time. Beyond that, they're given a discounted price for any additional hours that are needed.

Some VAs require a retainer to last for three or six months; I choose to use a month-to-month retainer. I know many VAs are successful at preselling blocks of time in five-hour increments—the more a client purchases at once, the lower the hourly rate is.

There are VAs who work on a flat hourly rate. If you do this, bill in advance. This method makes it harder for a VA to schedule their time. However, for some people, it works.

What advice do you have for managing your time and avoiding burnout?

Ennen: This is something you really need to focus on as a virtual assistant. On an ongoing basis, you need to track every minute of your time during your workday. If you wind up taking on too many clients too quickly and offer a 24-hour turnaround, for example, you will eventually burn out. Make sure you have it set up so you have time to get your work done, but still have time to yourself. Clients will ultimately want to see how much time you spent on each task or project that's assigned to you. Do not get into the habit of spending extra time working on a task or project that you don't bill for, just to keep your clients happy. The worst thing you could do is wind up working insane hours and not being paid for that work.

Eventually, you will come across clients who will complain about your work or your bill for the sole purpose of getting you to give them extra time for free. Don't fall into this trap. If you make a legitimate mistake, you need to fix it, often at your own expense. But if a client is trying to take advantage of you, don't allow them to.

In your experience, what are the points that need to be explicitly covered in the employment contract between a virtual assistant and their client?

Ennen: The contract needs to spell out all the specifics. It should describe the work that will be done, when it's due, what the client's expectations are, and what the VA's rate is, as well as how and when payment is due. There also needs to be a confidentiality clause built in. Everything should be clear and set in stone. If you've created a written proposal for your client, the key terms of the proposal should be repeated in the contract.

Erin Dahlquist, Latchkey Marketing

After spending many years as a marketing specialist in the sporting goods industry, Erin Dahlquist decided it was time for a career change. After moving to a rural area, she found her traditional job opportunities limited, so she began exploring ways she could work virtually while continuing to leverage her skill set and experience. She now divides her time between working as a virtual assistant and co-owning a digital marketing business, which she also does virtually.

To ensure she'd be able to bring in enough clients as a VA, she decided to work with an agency. While she admits she does not make as much as she would if she were operating her own virtual assistant business, Dahlquist likes having the agency find clients and handle all the bookkeeping and billing on her behalf. It's also consistent, reliable income and a fixed work schedule (in terms of time commitment), all of which keeps Dahlquist working for the VA agency.

Why did you decide to work with a virtual assistant agency?

Erin Dahlquist: It started out on a whim. I contacted the agency to obtain information and wound up deciding to work with them. The agency I work with has a unique way of matching up the right virtual assistant with the right client, so both parties consistently wind up happy. My focus is on providing general administrative assistance to clients, although I have the added marketing background that leads to some copywriting, blogging, and social media marketing-related tasks, in addition to handling scheduling or managing their email inbox.

If I decided that I wanted to give up my separate digital marketing agency and work full time as a virtual assistant, at that point I would definitely leave the agency I am working with and go independent. Of course, this would mean taking on all the responsibilities involved with operating my own business.

How do you define the role of a virtual assistant?

Dahlquist: It all depends on who you're working for. I try to put myself in their shoes and ask myself what I would want from a virtual assistant. Whatever will make their lives easier is the role I am going to step into.

To handle this job well, a virtual assistant needs plenty of self-discipline. They also need to be a self-starter, a great listener, and highly organized. When I see a need that my client has and that I can help fill, I make a point to tell them about it in a conversational—not a sales pitchy—way. I also try to see everything through the client's eyes, so I can help them not get bogged down in the minuscule day-to-day stuff.

What are your tricks for dealing with difficult or overly demanding clients?

Dahlquist: It's important to set boundaries at the beginning of the relationship. For example, I had a client who initially thought it was OK to consistently call me after my work hours and always expected me to be available to them. I needed to really spell out and reiterate my work hours and assure them that when they called after hours in the future, I would respond at the start of my next business day. If those terms don't work for the client, it's probably better that you don't work with that client.

What are some of the other boundaries you've had to set with clients?

Dahlquist: My work hours and when I am available to respond to clients are the biggest ones. I have also needed to limit how I used my digital marketing skills and experience when working as a virtual assistant, because the client would hire me for a less expensive task and then try to get me to handle high-end virtual marketing tasks that I'd typically charge much more money to perform. In this situation, I had to clarify with the client exactly what I was hired to do.

What is the one application that you rely on the most as a virtual assistant?

Dahlquist: It's called Clockify, and it's a highly flexible time tracker application. It allows me to manage my time accurately and then generate daily, weekly, or monthly reports for clients and the agency that showcase how every minute of my time was spent. As a virtual assistant, I could not live without this application.

I am a big advocate of time blocking, so I set aside specific amounts of time in my day to handle specific tasks or projects for clients. During their block of time, I only focus on that client's needs. I will close all other files, folders, and web browser windows and stay focused only on the task at hand. I use Clockify to schedule my time blocks and track how my time is ultimately spent. When I started working as a VA, I often forgot to take breaks during my workday, and I'd sometimes even skip lunch. Now I schedule multiple breaks and lunch into my daily schedule. During my breaks, I try to do something creative or relaxing to help me avoid burnout.

What tips can you share for building a long-lasting relationship with a client?

Dahlquist: I have had two of my clients for several years now, and I think the key to that long-term success is being a good listener whenever I am interacting with them. It's important to get to know your clients and really understand what they're saying.

For a relationship between a VA and client to work over the long term, there needs to be mutual respect. You don't need to become close friends, but you do need to develop a two-way relationship and understanding of each other's needs. If you don't achieve this mutual relationship, you're better off seeking out other clients.

How do you handle it when a client delegates a task to you but does not provide enough information about what needs to be done or how it should be done?

Dahlquist: I call this the rabbit hole effect. The way around this is to ask questions, ask more questions, and then ask follow-up questions until I get the clarity I need before moving forward. I would rather clarify exactly what the client wants at the start of a task or project than wind up making mistakes or not providing work that meets their expectations. As a virtual assistant, you can't be intimidated or afraid to ask questions.

What's one of the biggest mistakes you've seen up-and-coming virtual assistants make?

Dahlquist: Some people believe that because they're working from home and nobody is supervising them, they can goof off a lot and nobody will notice. In a normal office environment, for example, there is oversight for all the employees. This does not exist for virtual assistants working from home.

Virtual assistants are expected to handle all work that's assigned to them in a professional manner. They must complete tasks on time, be able to show how they spent their time, and constantly meet or exceed the expectations of their clients. There is no time or allowance for goofing off. If you are unable to work independently and maintain the self-discipline that's required, you are probably not cut out to be a virtual assistant or work remotely.

Felly Day, Felly Day VA

Felly Day spends much of her time traveling around the world as a backpacker. She works as a virtual assistant because she can handle all the work remotely and continue to earn a steady income while continuing her journeys.

Growing up in Canada, Day never went to university after graduating from high school. Instead, she worked a series of seasonal and hospitality jobs, mainly at ski resorts and hotels, where she landed during her travels.

At one point, she read a blog post that covered 20 ways to earn an income by working online; one of the career paths listed was a virtual assistant. Upon learning a bit more about what virtual assistants do, she went onto Upwork and began browsing listings for individuals and companies looking to hire a virtual assistant.

After landing her first few clients from Upwork, she began using Instagram as a marketing tool (username: @FellyDayVA) and has since found most of her clients through social media and her own website (https://fellyday.com/). At the time of this interview, Day had been based in Mexico for more than a year (mainly due to the COVID-19 pandemic). Her plan is to begin traveling again once she's able to do so safely.

What types of services do you offer to your clients?

Felly Day: I do a lot of content writing, email writing, virtual marketing, and copywriting for my clients. Writing has always been a passion for me. I have been a big fan of reading and writing my entire life. As a result of generating my own social media content as a digital nomad, my clients not only find me, but they also see firsthand a sampling of my work.

What would you say are the most important traits for a virtual assistant to possess?

Day: I am more on the creative side, as opposed to the admin side. While organization would be a key requirement for admin work, as someone who is paid to be creative, organization is not essential, nor is it one of my strong points. Individuals and companies hire me for my creative genius.

How important is it for a virtual assistant to create a brand for themselves?

Day: I'd have to say that it's much more important to have a unique brand voice and well-thought-out brand messaging than it is to have a logo or a flashy website. People hire people. Most of my clients hire me because they like me, even if there are 20 other people out there who could do the same caliber work for them. I strive to work with people who I mesh well with. Having a clear voice and message within my branding allows me to attract dream clients who relate to me and who I can easily relate to.

How many clients do you typically juggle at once?

Day: I typically juggle between six and 15 clients at once, but I now have a team of fellow VAs that I work with. Each of the VAs has a slightly different skill set. For example, one person is a graphic artist. Developing graphics is not something I am good at. If I were still working alone, I'd limit my client roster to just five or six at a time. At this point, I have created a virtual assistant agency, although initially it was a less structured agreement between me and the other VAs I work with. I personally find it challenging to manage other people, so it's more time-consuming than it should be. My passion is writing, and these days, I have the flexibility to only accept clients whose content I will really enjoy creating.

How do you adjust for the different time zones between you and many of your clients?

Day: When I set up my business, I knew this could be an issue, so I structured it around communicating with clients mainly via email and Slack, as opposed to by telephone or virtual meetings. With Slack, clients and my fellow VAs can message whenever they want, and I am able to respond as soon as I am available.

Right now, my clients are all in Canada and other parts of North America, and I am in Mexico. If there is a time difference, it's a small one. Soon I plan to travel through Europe, so this will create more of a time difference with my clients. Because of the way the business is structured, I don't anticipate this being a problem.

What strategy do you use to set your rates?

Day: I originally set an hourly rate for myself, and then eventually doubled it. Even once I doubled my rate, I am still charging well below market standards for the types of work I do. With most creative tasks, I found it works out much better to charge on a per-project basis, as opposed to an hourly rate.

These days, I work either on a per-project basis or using a monthly retainer model, depending on the project. For an email marketing campaign, I may have a three-month minimum retainer. I typically have my clients pay me in advance. Once the client and I agree on the work I will be doing, I send them a contract and invoice, and once the invoice is paid, I get to work.

I use a service called Dubsado to handle the management tasks associated with running my business. It includes the ability for clients to pay me via credit card or PayPal. For project management, I use Asana, and for messaging, I use Slack. I use Voxer to handle some virtual communication, and Clockify to track my time.

What are the most important pieces of equipment you use?

Day: Because I need to travel light, I rely exclusively on my internet-connected laptop computer and my smartphone.

What key pieces of information do you believe should be included in an employment contract between a virtual assistant and a client?

Day: The employment contract is important for defining and clarifying the business relationship. I created my contract myself and have needed to revise it on multiple occasions. One sticking point early on was a policy, which was discussed in advance, that prepurchased hours do not roll over from month to month. At first, this was not spelled out in the actual contract, and a client tried to fight me on this. I also needed to clearly spell out my hours of operation and availability once a client started messaging me at all hours of the day and night and expecting an instant response. The contract now states that emails and messages will not be answered after 5 P.M. eastern time. The contract should also spell out the terms of payment, applicable late fees, and cancelation policy.

Over the next three to five years, do you see the role of a virtual assistant expanding?

Day: Yes, definitely. I believe there will continue to be a fast-growing demand for virtual assistants with all sorts of specialties. It will also become a more common practice for companies of all sizes to hire virtual assistants. I think it will become common for a company to outsource HR, bookkeeping, and all sorts of project management-related tasks to a virtual assistant. I have seen firsthand the demand for virtual assistants with a specialty in website management, content creation, email marketing, and social media marketing grow considerably within the past year or so.

Vickie Hadge, Virtually Done by Vickie

Vickie Hadge has a degree in computer science and worked in the tech field early on in her career. In 1998, she had her first child. At that time, she wanted to be a stay-at-home mom until her child went to kindergarten. In 2002, however, she began looking into various work-from-home opportunities and discovered virtual assistants. To learn more about this opportunity, Hadge called a virtual assistant she found on the internet and began picking her brain.

Over the years, the two have become best friends. One of the first pieces of advice Hadge got was to join a networking group for VAs. By 2003, Hadge was ready to launch her own virtual assistant business.

How do you define the role of a virtual assistant?

Vickie Hadge: A virtual assistant is someone who supports their clients remotely. This can encompass many different areas of support. My particular niche is that I provide services related to Microsoft Office and Microsoft 365, as well as operations-type support to my clients.

What are the key personality traits needed to succeed as a virtual assistant?

Hadge: I think it's important to be able to connect with your clients and develop relationships with them. You can't hide behind your keyboard in your home office and avoid all forms of interaction with your clients. Communication skills are a must. A virtual assistant also needs to be organized, dedicated, and able to be highly productive working from a home office, despite the many distractions that can arise in this type of work environment.

People need to establish a dedicated place within their home to set up an office, and then stick to a regular work schedule. Knowing your personal skill set and continuously working to hone that skill set is important. For example, as someone who focuses on Microsoft Office and Microsoft 365, I need to stay up-to-date on the latest versions of each application within these suites, as the software is continuously evolving. Keeping up with the changes and updates in Word, PowerPoint, Excel, and Outlook is part of my job. This is time I invest into my company that allows me to maintain and expand my skill set.

How do you define your brand as a virtual assistant?

Hadge: My business name is Virtually Done by Vickie, so it incorporates my own name. People know they're hiring an individual—not an agency or faceless business entity. My brand is relationship-based. I have been doing this type of work for many years now, since 2003, so potential clients know they're hiring someone with experience and who is reliable. Branding your business is important if you're in this for the long haul.

It's important to narrow down your niche and focus in on the key services you offer to your clients, and then build your brand around that. Companies are not looking for people who can do anything. They're looking for people who can handle very specific tasks and who have experience and training related to that specialty.

When choosing what services to offer, make sure these are activities you really enjoy and that you won't get bored with too quickly. If you position yourself exclusively as an expert resume writer, for example, but you find writing resumes a boring and tedious task, you're going to hate your job and burn out quickly.

How do you market and promote your Virtually Done by Vickie business?

Hadge: My initial clients came from referrals I received from other VAs who I met in the networking groups, as well as from word-of-mouth referrals from clients. These days, I am very fortunate that I have a handful of clients I have been working with consistently for several years now, and I don't need to market my business to find new clients. I do, however, maintain a website for the business and stay active on LinkedIn, so potential new clients can find and contact me.

When I do need to land new clients, I find it's essential to be where my clients are. I attend professional talks and networking groups that are local and participate in Facebook groups online that cater to small business owners. I went to a professional talk at a local library a few years ago. When the guest speaker was finished, I walked up to her and handed her my business card. I quickly explained what I do and said that I might be able to help her if she was interested. A few months later, she contacted me on behalf of herself and her friend, and I wound up landing two long-term clients from that quick in-person interaction.

What are some of the biggest mistakes an up-and-coming virtual assistant should avoid?

Hadge: Taking on too much, too quickly can be a huge mistake. Also, don't accept clients you know will assign tasks to you that you won't enjoy doing. Find what you're passionate about and follow that passion, and don't promote yourself as someone who can do anything for anyone. Develop a niche as a virtual assistant so it's easier for potential clients to find you and understand exactly what you can offer to them.

One mistake I made early on was setting my rates too low. I also took on any kind of paying work, regardless of whether I would enjoy it. Another mistake is writing long emails and messages to your clients. If you have something long and complicated to say, make a phone call or get on a video call. Use messaging succinctly and get right to the point. You'll save yourself and your clients a lot of time. Brevity, as long as you're communicating clearly, will be appreciated by your clients.

What are some of the boundaries or ground rules you lay out for your clients in advance?

Hadge: I always make my typical business hours very clear. I let them know that during normal circumstances, I will respond within one business day. If they need me faster, or during nonbusiness hours, I have a specific procedure in place for how they should contact me, and I will charge them a higher rate. I also make it clear that I make every effort to do my work correctly, but it's the client's responsibility to double-check everything. If they find an error or omission, I will correct it.

What does a typical workday look like for you?

Hadge: I wake up every weekday morning around 6 A.M. I have coffee, read the news, check my social media, have breakfast, do some sort of exercise or meditation, work in my garden, and then get ready for work.

My workday is from 9 A.M. to 4 P.M. eastern time. At the start of my workday, I always check my work email and flag any emails that are important. I use Skype as a messaging tool with all my clients, so next I check my Skype threads to see and respond to any important new messages. I review my calendar for that day and prepare for any upcoming virtual meetings or phone calls, and then I continue by handling client tasks that I have prescheduled.

How do you think the work of virtual assistants will change over the next few years?

Hadge: I believe individuals and companies will use virtual assistants to handle a much wider range of tasks, many of which will require specialized skills. As a result, I think the term "virtual assistant" will continue to be used by people handling administrative tasks, but people offering specialized services will use more specialized titles, like "virtual bookkeeper," "virtual marketing specialist," or "virtual executive assistant." In my early years working as a virtual assistant, the term "stay at home secretary" was used a lot. These days, that term is obsolete.

Final Thoughts . . .

The concept of working from a home office for a variety of clients has been around for a long time. However, the technological advances of the past few years have made it possible to share data effortlessly via the internet and to truly collaborate in real-time online while working from home.

Virtual meeting technology, messaging services, file-sharing services, and other tools now allow virtual assistants to remotely handle a much broader range of tasks for a wider range of clients. This has translated into many more lucrative opportunities for virtual assistants.

While the COVID-19 pandemic was horrendous on many different levels, it did help convince business owners that remote work is a viable option and that businesses can succeed and grow by relying on virtual workers. Employers have also discovered they can save money by outsourcing certain tasks to virtual assistants rather than paying a full-time or part-time employee to handle those tasks.

One of the key advantages to becoming a virtual assistant is that you can launch your business relatively quickly and with a very small upfront investment, so the barriers to entry are practically nonexistent.

So if you think you have a skill set, education, and previous work experience that are in demand, and that would allow you to become a productive virtual assistant, there should be little stopping you from giving this career opportunity a try. To make your job even easier, be sure to use some of the software tools described in this book, and follow the advice offered in the interviews to avoid common pitfalls and mistakes.

There has never been a better time than right now to break into this line of work by launching your very own virtual assistant business!

Glossary

Administrative assistant: Someone who works in a traditional office assisting employees with a wide range of administrative tasks, such as filing, reception, dictation, scheduling, etc.

All-in-one multifunction printer: A laser or inkjet printer that also serves as a photocopier, scanner, and fax machine. This is a "must have" piece of equipment for anyone operating from a home office, as it saves space and handles multiple functions a virtual assistant will frequently require.

Boundaries: These are the limits a virtual assistant puts on their clients to ensure they're not mistreated or taken advantage of. A boundary might include specific business hours when they're available, or how a client should contact the virtual assistant. These stipulations are laid out during the onboarding process and usually included in the employment agreement.

Branding: The process of creating and showcasing your business in a way that will appeal to clients and convey its reputation. Branding should be extended across all online and real-world communications, including the company's website, letterhead, business cards, social media feeds, emails, invoices, brochures, and advertising.

Business plan: A document created as a business is first being established that provides a comprehensive summary of the business (including its goals) and details about the people running it. It also serves as a roadmap for helping the business leaders stay focused moving forward and can be used to attract potential investors.

Client onboarding: The process of establishing the business relationship between the virtual assistant and client. This typically involves at least a few initial phone calls or virtual meetings, outlining exactly what the virtual assistant will be doing and discussing how much the virtual assistant will be paid, as well as both parties signing an employment contract.

Clients: The individuals, businesses, or organizations that hire virtual assistants to work remotely and manage projects or perform specific tasks or activities on their behalf.

Cloud-based application: An application that's based entirely online rather than being saved on the user's computer or mobile device. The user typically gains access to the application through their web browser.

Communications skills: These are the most important skills a virtual assistant can possess. It involves their ability to communicate clearly, accurately, and succinctly, both verbally and in writing.

Cost of doing business: These are the expenses incurred by a business that don't necessarily get directly reimbursed by clients, such as the virtual assistant's phone bills, internet connectivity, marketing/promotional expenses, and equipment purchases.

Doing business as (DBA): A common type of legal business entity used by sole proprietors operating a virtual assistant business. It's the easiest type of business to set up from a legal and tax standpoint, but it offers fewer legal and financial protections than a limited liability company (LLC).

Domain name registrar: The online service that you use to register your company's domain name. Ideally, you want your domain name to be your company's name, ending with ".com" (i.e., www.YourCompanyName.com).

Elevator pitch: This is a marketing technique that involves being able to describe your business (in-person, on the phone, or online) in a succinct, clear, and engaging way to a prospective client. The concept is that you could complete the pitch during an elevator ride.

Email marketing: The process of sending email to prospective and existing clients to market your business and sell them your services. Spamming, however, is not recommended. This marketing technique works best when the recipients have opted into your email list, and when you include information the recipients perceive as valuable.

Executive assistant: In a traditional office environment, an executive assistant supports top-level executives by performing a wide range of administrative and organizational tasks. They're typically more experienced and have a broader skill set than a secretary or administrative assistant, and as a result, earn a higher income.

Facebook Business Page: The online presence created on Facebook for any business, which can be branded and transformed into an interactive community or used to communicate informally with prospective and existing clients by sharing various forms of multimedia content. Creating a Facebook Business Page is free. Go to https://www.facebook.com/business to learn more.

Facebook group: Facebook serves as the host to thousands of free Facebook groups (https://www.facebook.com/groups/discover), which are online special interest forums that provide a place for people with similar interests to interact in an informal way. Anyone can create a Facebook group, which can be open to the public or be an invitation-only (private) forum for a select few.

Freelancer: Someone who works independently to perform their specialized skills for an individual or company. They are a self employed independent contractor, not a part-time or full-time employee.

Hourly rate: The per-hour rate a virtual assistant charges their clients. This rate can vary based on the type of work being done or the number of hours at a time the virtual assistant is being hired for. Many virtual assistants have a published hourly rate, which they will discount when a client purchases a block of their time in advance. The hourly rate is typically based on what the virtual assistant will be doing, their skill set, their experience level, and the market value for that service.

Inbox management: This is a common task a virtual assistant is hired to perform for clients. It involves managing and organizing a client's email inbox, responding to certain messages on behalf of the client, flagging and prioritizing important messages that require the client's attention, and deleting spam.

Independent contractor: Someone, such as a virtual assistant, who is self-employed and works on a part-time (or temporary) basis for one or more clients.

Limited liability company (LLC): A type of legal business entity in the United States that many virtual assistants adopt once their company begins to grow. An LLC provides some legal protection for its owners but is easier to manage (from a legal and taxation standpoint) than other types of business entities. An LLC is assigned its own tax identification number (separate from the owner's Social Security number) and can have its own bank account under the company's name.

LinkedIn: This is a popular social media service (https://www.linkedin.com/), dedicated exclusively to business professionals and entrepreneurs and designed to promote professional networking. It offers messaging between members, a job board, free online training (covering a wide range of topics), and all sorts of how-to articles. The information on a LinkedIn profile is typically the same as on a resume. Businesses can also have their own LinkedIn page that can be used for marketing and promotional purposes.

Messaging (aka instant messaging or IM): The ability for two or more people to communicate via short text messages, either from a mobile device or a computer. There are messaging services that cater primarily to businesses, like Slack, although IM is also a widely used feature on most social media services and virtual meeting platforms. Messaging is a popular way for virtual assistants to communicate with their clients, and it is secure, fast, and convenient.

Mission statement: A short summary outlining a company's objectives, philosophy, and overall purpose.

Mobile app: A program (aka application) designed to run specifically on a mobile device, such as a smartphone or tablet. For the Apple iPhone and iPad, mobile apps can be found and installed through the App Store. Android-based mobile device users can find and download apps from the Google Play Store.

Mobile device: A smartphone or tablet that can connect to the internet via wifi or a cellular data service to perform a wide range of tasks. These are "must have" tools for virtual assistants as they allow for work to be done away from a home office or desktop computer.

Networking: For the purposes of a virtual assistant, this is the process of introducing yourself and communicating with other people (e.g., friends, family members, past co-workers, people attending a trade show/industry gathering/chamber of commerce meeting, etc.) to share details about your business and generate new client prospects.

Niche: While a virtual assistant can be a jack-of-all-trades and offer a broad range of services to their clients, it's often easier to land clients by establishing a niche or specialization.

VAs with a specific skill set, experience, and education are typically able to charge premium rates for performing highly specialized tasks or services for clients.

Office suite: A collection of applications that perform a wide range of tasks that are typically used in a work environment, including word processing, spreadsheet management, digital slide presentations, and email management. The most popular office suites include Microsoft Office (or Microsoft 365), Google Workspace, Apple iWork, and Apache OpenOffice.

Package: For the purposes of a virtual assistant, a package refers to a block of time (such as 5, 10, or 20 hours) that a client prepurchases, often at a discounted rate. Unused hours can either expire at the end of the month or roll over to the next billing period.

Payment terms: This stipulates how and when a virtual assistant will be paid by the client. It's agreed to in advance (during the onboarding process) and described clearly in the virtual assistant employment contract.

Press release: Typically a one- or two-page document formatted in a specific way, which is used to communicate a newsworthy message from a company to members of the working media (e.g., newspapers, magazines, TV shows, radio programs, bloggers, and podcasters). Press releases are used as part of a company's overall PR efforts to generate editorial coverage and earn free publicity.

Professional association: An organization that caters to people working in a specific field or industry. The International Association of Professional Virtual Assistants (IAPO), The International Virtual Assistants Association (IVAA), and the Association of Virtual Assistants (AVA) are examples of professional associations targeted to virtual assistants. These organizations typically offer networking opportunities, training and certification programs, job listings, industry standards, and discounts on commonly used products or services.

Public relations (PR): A marketing strategy used by individuals and companies to promote themselves in the media (in the form of editorial coverage), without having to pay for advertising. A company might use PR to get one of their leaders interviewed or profiled, to get products or services reviewed or promoted, or to have a company spokesperson used as an expert source for a news story. PR efforts often target journalists who cover a specific subject for TV, radio, print, or electronic media (including blogs and podcasts).

Retainer fee: An advance payment made by a client to an independent contractor, which is considered a down payment for services in the future. A retainer might be used when the client is not sure how much of a virtual assistant's time they'll require during a particular billing cycle, so they prepay for a bunch of hours and then receive an invoice for the remaining time used at the end of a billing cycle.

Scheduling/calendar management: This is a common task a virtual assistant is hired to perform for clients. It involves managing all aspects of a client's calendar, including scheduling their meetings and phone calls.

Self-employed: Someone who works for themselves and operates their own business.

Services menu: A comprehensive list and description of the services a virtual assistant offers their clients. This menu is a marketing and sales tool that should be featured prominently on a virtual assistant's website, in promotional emails, and in brochures. The goal is to entice clients to consider all the ways a virtual assistant could potentially benefit a prospective client and showcase additional ways they could be helping existing clients.

Social media marketing: The use of social media platforms, such as Facebook, Twitter, Instagram, LinkedIn, TikTok, and Pinterest, to target a specific audience and promote a business and its services.

Time management: The tool set used by a virtual assistant to manage their time properly and productively, so they can work efficiently and be available to handle all the tasks, projects, and activities required to manage their own business and cater to the needs and demands of their clients.

Time tracker application: Software used to track every minute of a virtual assistant's time when they're actively working on behalf of a specific client. A time tracker application will keep track of how much time is spent on each task, activity, or project, and generate informative reports for clients.

VA: A commonly used abbreviation for virtual assistant.

Video call: A way to communicate with one or more people remotely by using the camera, microphone, and speaker(s) built into any internet-connected computer or mobile device. Participants can both see and hear those involved in the call.

Virtual assistant: A self-employed person who performs tasks for a client remotely (typically from a home office). A virtual assistant can be hired to handle general or specific administrative tasks, serve as a remote phone receptionist, or perform more specialized tasks for clients, like bookkeeping, website development, content creation, or social media marketing.

Virtual assistant agency: An agency that serves as the middleman between virtual assistants and clients. In exchange for a percentage of the virtual assistant's income (typically 40 to 50 percent), an agency will find and secure clients for a virtual assistant and then handle all billing, payment, and client management tasks. The virtual assistant is responsible only for performing the specific tasks or activities the client needs them to handle, typically on a per-hour basis.

Virtual assistant employment contract: The written contract between a virtual assistant and a client that outlines the scope of what the virtual assistant is being hired to do. The contract includes a list of services to be provided, rates, payment terms, and when the virtual assistant will be available to the client (their business hours).

Virtual assistant software: This is specialized software, such as Adminja or HoneyBook, designed to provide a wide range of tools for managing a virtual assistant business. Time tracking, scheduling, invoice management, client management (CRM), and project/task management are all typically integrated into these applications.

Virtual meeting: An online meeting where a group of people who are working from different locations can interact in real-time using video, audio, and text messaging simultaneously. Popular virtual meeting services used by virtual assistants (and their clients) include Zoom, Skype, Microsoft Teams, GoToMeeting, Google Meet, Webex by Cisco, and Zoho Meeting.

Virtual receptionist: Someone who works remotely for an individual or company to answer and transfer incoming calls, take messages, and give information to callers based on scripts or protocols provided by the client. This is one of several tasks a virtual assistant is often hired to perform for clients.

Voice call: A traditional phone call where two or more people in separate locations communicate using audio only.

Voice over Internet Protocol (VoIP): Technology available to computer, smartphone, and tablet users that allows people to make and receive voice calls and video calls, participate in virtual meetings, and communicate in real-time via messaging using the internet.

About the Author

Jason R. Rich (https://jasonrich.com/) is an accomplished author, journalist, and photographer. Some of his recently published books for Entrepreneur Press include:

- ▶ *Start Your Own Etsy Business*

- ▶ *Start Your Own Import/Export Business*

- ▶ *Start Your Own Photography Business*

- ▶ *Start Your Own Podcast Business*

- ▶ *Start Your Own Travel Hosting Business*

- ▶ *Start Your Own Virtual Assistant Business*

- ▶ *Ultimate Guide to YouTube for Business, Second Edition*

- ▶ *Ultimate Guide to Shopify for Business*

As a journalist, Jason's articles appear in a wide range of national magazines, major daily newspapers, and popular websites, including *AARP the Magazine*, AARP.org, and PawTracks.com. He is also a consumer technology staff writer for *Forbes Vetted* (www.Forbes.com/vetted). You can listen to his podcast, *Jason Rich's Featured App of the Week* (http://www.featuredapppodcast.com/), on Apple Podcasts and a variety of other popular podcast services.

Throughout parts of the year, Jason travels around the world lecturing about digital photography, mobile devices, internet security, and consumer electronics aboard cruise ships operated by several major cruise lines, including Carnival Cruise Line. You can follow his travel adventures and learn more about his latest writing and photography projects by following him on Facebook (JasonRich7), Instagram (@JasonRich7), Twitter (@JasonRich7), and LinkedIn (JasonRich7).

Index

CPSIA information can be obtained
at www.ICGtesting.com
Printed in the USA
JSHW030141241022
31966JS00007B/5